The
TRANSITION
MINDSET

amplifypublishing.com

The Transition Mindset
How Retiring from the NFL at the Peak
of My Career Changed My Life

For more information, please contact:
Amplify Publishing, an imprint of Amplify Publishing Group
620 Herndon Parkway #320
Herndon, VA 20170
info@amplifypublishing.com

CPSIA Code: PRFRE0322A
Library of Congress Control Number: 2021922756
ISBN-13: 978-1-64543-652-2

Printed in Canada

This book is dedicated to my mom,
for pushing me to be great and
always being there for me.

THE
TRANSITION
MINDSET

How Retiring from the NFL
at the Peak of My Career
Changed My Life

Andre Hal

CONTENTS

FOREWORD

Romeo Crennel

HOUSTON TEXANS INTERIM HEAD COACH

There isn't anyone in the world like Andre Hal. Forget the fact that he is one of the very few NFL players who were drafted in the seventh round and then went on to sign a multimillion-dollar contract. Forget the fact that he survived cancer and returned to play later that same year. Forget that he retired at the age of twenty-six, when he had many years of great football ahead of him.

Seriously, leave all that behind, and there is still so much about Dre that is incredible and maybe even defies belief. He was the last player the Houston Texans selected in the 2014 draft, but when he showed up for camp, you could tell by the way he carried himself that he was confident about what he was going to be able to bring to the table and to the team. You could just tell he knew his value. Like most rookies in a new environment, you have veterans in front of you, so you have to establish yourself somehow. He was willing to do whatever it took to get that foothold. That meant playing special teams—that is, the kickoff and punting units—and I know he played there in college a bit, but a lot of times, starters in college, when they get to this level, consider special teams as being beneath them. Not Dre Hal, though. He knew he needed to develop a role for himself to make the team. He showed a willingness to do whatever we wanted and whatever we asked to show that he belonged and that he would be able to help.

When Dre joined us in Houston, he was a cornerback, and there were several guys ahead of him on the depth chart. We all knew it was going to be very hard for him to crack the starting lineup and even to make the team right off. He knew it too. But he *still* had that confidence; he still held that strong belief that he was good enough to make it and would earn his place on the team. That confidence, combined with his work ethic, his knowledge of the game, and his sharp instincts, were the things that allowed him to get through that rookie year and earn himself a second year.

Because of what he showed us that first year, we felt that moving him to safety might be the best bet for him and also the best bet for us, especially since that position had been tricky for the team. We were continually looking for guys who could fill that position in our system; not everyone can. You have to be a communicator, you have to be able to take control, to relate to your teammates, and to recognize other defenses in ways a cornerback doesn't have to. There's more responsibility involved, and not everyone can handle it. When we moved Dre to the position, he took the bull by the horns, just like we knew he would. He became that dependable force on the back end for us. It really impressed us how he approached it, and he almost immediately became a much bigger, more important part of the defense. Not a lot of players would have been willing to make that switch, especially after playing their whole career as cornerback, but Dre understood that this was his path to establish himself.

I didn't know Dre before we drafted him, though I did have some familiarity with his school, Vanderbilt, because I'd gone to Western Kentucky University, an hour drive north of Nashville, in Bowling Green, Kentucky. Just the fact that he graduated from Vandy, knowing its excellent academic reputation, grabbed my attention. As we talked during the rookie camp and began to get to know each other, there was definitely a common bond. I didn't just like Dre; I respected him, and I appreciated the way he conducted himself and carried himself during his time with the team. We didn't just need his athletic ability—we needed his attitude, his brain, his strong leadership on the field, and his quiet leadership off of it. We needed everything that he was, everything that he brought to the game and to the team. All of this is what led to him signing that big contract, which he earned and deserved.

When you talk about a seventh-round pick, a lot of times that guy has some things that you're looking for, so you take a chance on him. We'll take his height, weight, speed, we'll take his ability, and then see how he adapts. How he fits. *If* he fits. Will he be a good pro? Is he going to pay attention in the meetings? Is he going to work on the field? Because not all of them pay attention. Not all of them do whatever it takes or take the job seriously.

What I learned about Andre Hal is that he takes everything seriously. He was serious about the game and about his part in it. He made a real impact on the defensive backs coach, on the special teams coach, and he made a big impact on *me*. We're always looking for smart, tough, dependable guys. We feel like these are the guys who will make our unit better. That's true for any job but especially for football. The qualities Dre brought to the table made him that much more valuable. He had that willingness to try to be the best that he could be and learn everything he needed to learn to succeed. That's why, when he came to me that day in April 2019 and told me he was retiring from football, I knew he was going to be okay because I knew that he would do everything possible to succeed outside of the game.

He went through cancer, he got back on the field, and I think in doing that, he was able to fulfill a drive within himself. He showed that, "Boom, I can do it. I did it. I'm back on the field. So now, what else is there? I've played five years in the league as a seventh-round draft choice. What else do I want to do in my life?" For me, there was nothing else to do but just support him. Knowing Dre, I knew that he must have thought it out and thought it through, so why should I try to change his mind?

So many players come through the life of a coach, and you try to treat them equally because you never want to show favoritism. But there are some positions and some guys that you have a better relationship with. Someone playing Dre's position, with him being the signal caller on the back end of the defense and my depending on him to make the correct call to get the guys lined up and then still play the game, you develop a trust. As a coach, you learn to depend on this guy because you know he's going to do his very best every time the ball is snapped. You don't develop that same relationship with every position or every player, but with Andre, there was a bond. There still is.

Dre's strong work ethic, his drive to succeed, to always be the best he could possibly be, I knew that would translate to the real world. While I was sorry to lose him, I knew that he had made up his mind and that I couldn't talk him out of it, but I also knew that I shouldn't even try. Andre is his own man, very self-possessed, and that quality makes him formidable. It made him formidable as a football player, and it makes him formidable as a businessman. I knew that Dre would manage his transition with grace, style, and confidence because that's who Dre is.

When I first got into the league, there weren't that many Black coaches. But since the majority of the players are Black, I kind of felt like I needed to be an example for the players so that they would have the opportunity to fulfill their hopes and dreams. Many of them have had issues at home, or might not have had a father at home, for example, and now they're looking to someone to help fill that role. I'm with these guys all the time, most of the day, for six or seven months out of the year, sometimes more. They know that if they want to talk or if they need guidance or advice, they always have the opportunity to come and get it. That's the sort of role that I've taken on, and because of my longevity in the league, I think it helps players see me more as a father figure. Word gets around that Coach Crennel will shoot you straight.

Sometimes, with certain players, I get to establish a closer relationship. Once Dre established himself as the starting safety, we began to develop a stronger bond, but when he told me that it was time for a change, that it was time for him to move on and try something new, I understood. I was a bit surprised, of course, because he'd come back so strong after the cancer, but I got it. He knew it was time to do something else with his life, something different, and not only did I not want to stand in his way, I wanted to support him. I continue to support him and want what's best for him. It's his life, and he's got to live it the best way he can. From what I can see, that's exactly what he's doing.

As a coach, you lose players all the time. Sometimes on a weekly basis. It goes with the job. So losing a player is something I'm used to, even if it's a good guy who I depend on. But if that kind of guy makes a decision like the one Andre has made, then I already know it wasn't a snap decision. I know he spent some time thinking it through. That's how Dre is.

If anyone can write a book about positive mindsets and successful transitions, it's Dre. He takes both things very seriously, and I'm sure we'll learn a lot from him here— valuable lessons that we can apply in our own lives. I am very proud of Andre. I think you will be, too.

CHAPTER 1

Retirement

I opened my eyes and wondered for yet another morning, *Is this my last day as a pro football player?*

It was a beautiful spring day, Tuesday, April 2, 2019, and I'd been struggling with this decision for months. Ever since my father died six months earlier in October, I'd found that my love of football had suffered. My entire life, I'd equated playing football with my father's love. He and my mom split when I was about nine, and after that, he wasn't around a whole lot. Unless there was a game. Then I knew he'd be there, so I kept playing. Through peewee and high school, college, all the way to the pros. I was one of those rare men who made it all the way to the top, the starting safety on an NFL team. And not just any team—the Houston Texans. A playoff team. Because I was fast and strong and talented, and thanks at least partially to that desire to connect with a father who was barely there, I had reached the highest level an athlete can reach.

But here's the thing: football had always meant much more to him than it ever did to me. I enjoyed football, but I saw it as a means to an end. For me, it had always been about connecting with him on the one hand and setting up my future on the other. The two of us had a very complicated relationship, and football was at the center of it. Always had been.

Now, suddenly, he was gone, and he'd taken my love of the game with him. It just took me a while to figure that out.

At first, I'd thought I was just mourning his passing, but as the season continued, I found it harder and harder to gear up for games, and the doubts crept in. When you're a professional athlete, doubt is the enemy. You have to believe that you're the best, that you belong, and that this is what you want to do. It's too hard otherwise. There are too many others who want your job. The physical aspect is already brutal enough, *especially* in football, so if the doubts start creeping in or the love isn't there, what's the point? Mindset matters.

Say you're twenty-six years old, a professional athlete just reaching your physical prime, and you've just signed a contract that has made you a millionaire several times over. People your age don't just *retire*. They're just getting started. If you even admit to others that you're thinking about it, they'll call you crazy. But here I was, thinking that maybe, somehow, I'd reached the end.

For the weeks and months since the season had ended on a cold January night, I'd been thinking about it, but I still hadn't been able to come to a decision. I knew the clock was ticking. Soon, organized team activities (OTAs) would start up, and the team was getting ready for the annual NFL draft.

I knew that if I went back to participate in OTAs, there would be no getting out of it. No way. OTAs are the first practices back after several months off. The way the NFL works is you basically beat the hell out of your body on the field for four months, then you have roughly four months to recover, both physically and mentally, before it starts up again in May with light workouts before full training camp opens in July. The first OTAs are generally easier, but it's as much about being back with the team as anything else. It's about the camaraderie, being with the guys, and getting back into the swing of things.

It's also about the *mindset* of being back that makes the difference. Being in the right headspace counts. It's about getting yourself back into that football mentality. Being away from the game for months means letting yourself think of other things, developing other interests and pursuits. But once the season starts up again, it's all football all the time. When you're fully involved in the game, when it's all you're about and takes your total focus, that's fine. But when that focus begins to get fuzzy, when other things intrude on it, or if you're not fully committed, then it's time to take a look in the mirror. That's what I had been doing since the season ended without coming to a decision.

But if I returned for the first round of OTAs, I knew I would be back, and I would stay back whether I wanted to or not. That sounds strange, doesn't it? Like I wouldn't have any choice in the matter? I should be able to walk away any time I want, right? No one was exactly twisting my arm to stay in the

NFL. But it's not quite that simple. You can't just walk away. It's not a switch you can turn on or off. No, that switch has got to be on all the time. That's what my struggle was about—my inability to be "on" when "off" might have felt better.

Coming back to team workouts, though, putting on the helmet, being around the guys, being outside and running around like I had my entire life, that would get me back into it, at least in the beginning. Over time, though, I would grow to regret it.

Can you imagine that? Regretting being a part of a pro football team? Even being torn about it? In the 2018 season, because of injuries, I'd only played eight of sixteen games and still tied for the team lead in interceptions, with three. So it wasn't like I had somehow lost my ability or wasn't good enough anymore. I was still worth every penny of the fifteen-million-dollar contract I'd signed a year and a half earlier.

I just wasn't sure I wanted to put myself through it any-more, especially since my heart clearly wasn't in it.

The only reason why this should have been troublesome is that, well, on the surface, it didn't make any sense. I had a great contract, was making a lot of money, liked my team-mates, and had the kind of career that most people could only dream of. My fifth season with the Texans had come to an end on January 5, 2019, in a 21–7 upset loss to the Indi-anapolis Colts in the first round of the playoffs. For my last four years with the team, I had been one of two starting safe-ties, and in three of the previous four years, we had won the AFC South division title (with one lousy year mixed in when we only won four games).

But I wasn't happy. And I hadn't been for a long time. Over the course of those last few months, I had explored lots of other things that had nothing to do with football to see what else was out there for me. I think this is what a lot of people do when they want to make a change, when they're ready to transition to something new. Maybe it's transitioning out of a job or a relationship or a living situation—it could be anything—but there's just a natural desire to see what else is out there, to see what's next. It's like the old saying about the devil you know versus the devil you don't: You may not like your current situation, but what if the new one you choose is even worse? What then? You end up regretting that you left a situation you didn't even like instead of being happy that you took the step to make it better. Even if it didn't work out this time, at least now you know that you can do it, and the next time will hopefully be an improvement.

On that morning of April 2, though, from the moment I opened my eyes, I was pretty sure I was done. I might not have been 100 percent certain, but I knew it was wearing on me, and I knew I had to make a decision. I also knew that if I went back, I'd *stay* back, no two ways about it. So here's what I did that morning:

I got up and went through my normal morning routine. I brushed my teeth and I meditated. I'd been meditating for a while now, and it had helped me through a bunch of stuff, some of it football related, some not. Meditation was about more than organizing my thoughts and calming myself down—it was about stillness. Being able to take a moment and focus. In this case, focusing on a problem that involved my lack of focus.

On that day, when I meditated, I made sure I used meditation differently than I normally do. Normally, I don't think of anything and let my mind rest. Let things go, and allow it to think about what it wants to think about. But this time I forced myself to think about retiring, why I was doing it, so I could get it straight in my head and explain it to my coaches. Even though I'd been thinking about it and was pretty sure I was going to walk away from the game, at that moment, I still didn't really have a definite reason for why.

I'd gotten into meditation because I'd read that it kept the mind engaged in the things you're doing. Originally, I did it to help my game, to give me an advantage, but of course that changed as my priorities did. As I meditated on it that morning, suddenly, finally, it became clear. My dad came to mind, and I thought about the time we spent together and how it was almost always about football. Football. But he's not here anymore, so why do it? Right then I knew. I couldn't do it anymore because he's not here anymore, and I no longer had any reason to pursue it.

Hard as it might be to believe, while I knew I'd always associated the game with my dad, it was the first time I'd really connected with the fact that my passion for the game was so directly tied to him. I'd felt my love for the game vanish the moment my dad died, but I finished out the season anyway, at least partially because I couldn't find the words to explain it, even to myself. I couldn't come to terms with the idea that "If he's not here, then the game just doesn't mean the same thing to me. If he's not here, I just can't do it anymore."

It was there as an intangible thing, but I just couldn't wrap my head around it because I was mourning my father.

But that April morning, suddenly it was all clear. That's when the decision was made. *I was done.* No doubt about it, I was walking away from football.

And just like that, I felt a weight lift off my shoulders. I felt a sense of euphoria, of genuine joy, and also a sense of relief that I had made a decision I was proud of and that I knew I could stand behind. Even if it was what others would consider the wrong decision, I knew it was the right one for me. And I knew it immediately and instinctively.

Sure, there would be others who would definitely think it was the wrong decision. Many others, in fact. Maybe even most people. They would think I was crazy. Some might even be angry at me, to be willing to walk away from something that so many others desperately wanted. Being an NFL player is the dream of countless young men, and here I was, willfully deciding not to do it anymore—not in my thirties, as I approached the natural end of the line, but in my prime, when I still conceivably had years ahead. I knew that plenty of people would call me crazy and ungrateful. But I wasn't any of those things. In fact, I was maybe the most sane I've ever been.

It also occurred to me that I'd made the subconscious decision to wait a day to make this decision—until April 2—because I was afraid that if I'd done it on April 1 people might think I was pulling an April Fool's prank. But on the second? No chance.

What did I do first? I called my agent, Tony Paige. Tony had been with me since I graduated from Vanderbilt University. I said, "Yeah, I'm done. I'm about to retire." He didn't believe me at first, but I laid it out for him, plain and simple:

"Yeah, I really see it right now. I'm about to retire. I don't feel like playing anymore. I don't feel it in the morning, the love, the goal, none of it."

We talked for about thirty minutes as he prodded me, tried to talk me into just going back for OTAs, see how I felt about it, but I told him what I'd already figured out: that if I went back for that, I'd never leave. We reminisced about my time playing football. He reminded me of all the good times I'd had, like the interception I returned for a touchdown against Jacksonville in 2015 (known in the game as a "pick six"), and the time I intercepted Tom Brady—probably the greatest quarterback of all time—in a 2017 playoff loss and how rewarding the game had been for me. I don't know if he was really trying to get me to go back into it or if he was kind of feeling me out to see if I was serious or not. But when I just kept my ground, stayed serious, and was insistent that this was what I wanted, he said he understood and that I needed to get in touch with the Texans' general manager, Brian Gaine. I told Tony I'd call him, but he insisted I go see him and tell him in person.

Looking back on it, I think he might have thought that a face-to-face meeting could cause me to change my mind, because, you know, it's some pretty scary stuff to go tell your boss that you don't want to play the game anymore. That's a scary thing for *anybody* to do—it's as intimidating as breaking up with someone—plus, I still had a contract with the team. I was about to leave six or seven million dollars on the table and a big hole in the team's defense. But I also believe that you should never ignore what your gut tells you. In fact, when the world is yelling the loudest is when you should listen to your gut the most closely.

I called Brian, asked if I could come see him. He told me he couldn't talk right then because they had so much going on with the draft only a couple weeks away. But when I texted him and told him I'd made the decision to retire and I just wanted to tell him to his face rather than over the phone, he called me right back and said, "Yeah. You'd better come in."

I got in my car and drove over to NRG Stadium. I only live ten minutes away, so it was a quick trip. I was nervous about it, but I also knew I had to do this. That it was time.

So I pulled into the stadium parking lot. Sat in my car for a minute. Took a few deep breaths and said to myself, "I'm really going to do this. I'm really about to retire, aren't I?" I'd already moved into my transition mindset; I knew it was the right decision. "This is it," I said to myself as I got out of the car. I walked into Brian's office, sat down, and gave it to him straight. I told him all the things I've already mentioned: that it just wasn't in me anymore, that after my dad passed, I had no love for the game, how all that love had just vaporized when he died, and how I didn't have the drive or the desire to go out there anymore. I also told him that, while thinking about it, I realized I'd only finished the season because I didn't want to let the team down.

When you're working your butt off but you find you're doing it for the wrong reason, it's time to find the right reason. This is true in any line of work, any walk of life, but it is especially true in football. Pushing myself to keep my body in top shape had, for so long, been about being able to play the game. Squatting 350 pounds, making myself superhumanly strong, all of the contact—which, to be honest, I never liked all that much anyway—working on the field and watching film, doing what I could to improve, I did all of that so that I could do my job better, and it had paid off. But on the flip side, my back hurt, my knees hurt, my left shoulder hurt, my ankles hurt, *everything* hurt…all the time. I had taken my body for granted, putting it through so much.

Lately, though, I'd been focusing more on staying in shape for *me*, for my own sake, not just for the game. My body was feeling better, nothing was hurting, and I had no great interest in putting it through all that again. I explained all this to Brian. I told him that I'd been thinking about this for a long time and that since I'd come to an understanding about it all, I knew this was the right decision.

What do you think was his first response? If your guess was, "Try to get me to stay for OTAs to see how I feel," give yourself a prize, because that's exactly what he did. Not that I didn't appreciate it, because he clearly wanted me to stay on the team, and that means a lot, but my mind was made up. Brian said, "We love you here, Dre," and "We want you to be part of the team." You know, all the standard stuff. We went back and forth for a few minutes, and then it was over, and I went to find my head coach, Bill O'Brien.

Bill was shocked. I told him pretty much the same stuff I'd told Brian, but Bill had a slightly different reaction. He wanted to know why I hadn't come in to talk to him about it. I explained to him that I had wanted to make the decision myself *first*, without having anyone trying to sway me one way or the other. This was going to be my decision, and mine alone.

This is true off the field too: If you're about to announce or share a major decision, try to make sure you've come to that decision on your own first. Be clear about it in your own mind so people don't try to shift your thinking or cause you to doubt yourself. I knew I didn't want to go back and forth about my decision with other people. Anyone who knows me well knows that I'm a serious guy, and once I say I'm going to do something, I stick to it. I didn't want to be convinced or cajoled. That's why I didn't tell anybody until I did it.

Bill said all the right things. How much they were going to miss me, how much he loved having me on the team and what a good teammate I was, and that he understood. That left me with one more major conversation, and this one was, for me, the biggest.

The Texans' defensive coordinator was Romeo Crennel. We call him "Rac," and he's a father figure to his players. Without question, he's one of the best coaches I've ever had in my life. This is the NFL. It's a business. But he always treated us like we were *people* first. He's the defensive coordinator, and he's the one who decides who's going to play, but he always made sure that you knew that he saw you as a man. Especially as a Black man.

Again, I was a Black man in the NFL, with a lot of other Black men, many of them coming from families either without a father or, like me, one who wasn't around much. So Rac was a father figure to a lot of the Black men in the room. If somebody had a problem, we'd go to him. He's wise. He's been through a lot and went out of his way to share that with the men who played for him. A great coach, yes, but more than that, Romeo is a great man, and the last thing I wanted to do was disappoint him. He was the one, after all, who helped make me the player I became. When I switched positions from cornerback to safety (and I'll get to that soon enough), he was the one who saw how hard I was working and how much I wanted it and said, "Andre deserves a chance." He was always on my side, and I realized as I was walking to his office that I was more nervous about talking to him about my decision than I was about talking to anyone else.

But when I got to his office and told him my plan to walk away from the game, he just wrapped me in a big hug. He understood. It was that simple.

The rest of it was pretty easy. My defensive backfield coach, Anthony Midget, wasn't at the stadium, so I just called him, and he congratulated me and wished me luck, told me I'd had a great career and to stay in touch. I swung by the training room and said goodbye to the trainers who had helped me stay on the field throughout my various injuries. Every player spends a ton of time in that room and working with that squad, and it was nice to shoot the breeze with them a bit on my way out. They were as surprised as everyone else was but just as supportive.

Next, I went to the locker room to clean out my locker, and J. J. Moses, who was then the team's head of player engagement, swung by to chat. I took my time with my locker because J. J. and I spent close to an hour laughing and reminiscing. J. J.'s a former player too, and he also understood why I was walking away.

Then it was time to leave. As I walked out of the stadium for the last time, my personal possessions in a bag, people stopped me, wondering what I was doing. Had I been cut?

Had the team released me? No, I said, I had retired. I was done with football. Everyone was stunned, because a guy like me—twenty-six years old, at the top of his game, desired by the team, his whole career still in front of him—just doesn't retire.

Honestly, every time I said it—that I was *retiring*—I surprised myself too. Every time I said it, it was hammered home a bit more. I got to my car and looked up at the stadium. I was done. I was retired. Just like that, it was over. And you know what?

I felt free.

I knew the news was going to break soon, and I wanted to be home and away from everyone else when it did. I picked up some food and headed back to my house, and on the way, it dawned on me that, for the first time, *I could just be myself.* It's not like football was an act—I mean, you obviously have to work your butt off—but it is entertainment, and there is a little bit of acting involved.

To be clear, it wasn't that I was walking away from the hard work. I work hard every day of my life, but now I could back off and just sort of focus on me for a minute. When I played football, I had to worry about everybody. Not just my coaches and teammates but feeling the need to take care of my family too. Making sure everybody was okay. But that gets old, and I found myself thinking, "I wish everyone would just leave me alone and let me process this myself." Finally, after all these years, I was taking time to focus on Andre.

That feeling of freedom I felt when I left the stadium only grew stronger as the day went on. I'd felt so much pressure for so long, especially after I'd signed that big contract a year and a half earlier (and I'll get to that too). At the time, I had a lot of people coming to me with their hands out to see what they could get off me and to "share" in my success. Now, with me retiring, that source of stress would go away, and I could be a regular person. At that moment, it was all I wanted. To be regular.

I still remember the feeling as clearly as if it happened yesterday. Like a bolt of lightning, it all hit me: "Man, you're finally out. You're done. You're free. You can be you. You don't have to wake up every morning and work out for a team, now you can work out for yourself, for your own well-being. You can stay in shape just to be healthy. You're not trying to get super strong, be super fast, to run around a football field, and try to tackle a 250-pound running back. You can just be yourself."

Sitting at home, waiting for the news to break, I found myself thinking about everything that had just happened. Walking away from the game was not something I'd ever thought I would do. Football was my life. It was all I'd ever done, even if, looking back, it was for the wrong reasons. Walking in and telling the GM and the head coach and the defensive coordinator that I was done seemed a little insane to me. It seemed insane to a lot of people. But I did it.

I could feel I'd already transitioned into a different person. This whole experience, everything that went into this decision, the old Dre *never* would've done it. The work I'd done on myself, with meditation and mindfulness, and the awareness of my place in the game and in the world, gave me a new mindset about what I can do and who I can be. It was an awakening. Even as I went through all the pros and cons and the decision-making about whether I was going to keep playing, even when I was practicing yoga and meditating and being spiritual, the awakening didn't actually hit me until after I'd officially walked away from football. After I'd told people what I was doing, after I'd looked my coaches in the eye, only then did I fully realize how trapped I'd felt the whole time I was playing. I had restricted myself to one thing my whole life—the game—and now that I was out, there were so many possibilities, so many options for me and my future.

This is the kind of thing that happens all the time, every day, in all parts of the world and all walks of life. People realizing that they've been restricted, that they're doing the wrong thing, and that they aren't happy. Don't get me wrong, I was no prisoner. I knew I was doing what others dreamed of and was getting paid really well to do it, but life and happiness and fulfillment are about much more than that, no matter where you are or what you do for a living.

I was proud of myself, and I suddenly felt transformed. I was transitioning into a whole new life, a whole new way of being, and, for the first time, I felt ready for it.

I texted a few of my teammates to let them know what had happened, then I turned on ESPN, and pretty soon I saw my own name on the crawl along the bottom of the screen. If it hadn't hit home already, it sure did then. If for no other reason than that I realized that this was the last time I would ever see my name show up on the ticker, simply because I was no longer someone ESPN would cover. I couldn't be. I wasn't a pro athlete anymore. I'd been playing for so long, and while I felt like I was losing something, I also felt that I was gaining something at the same time: freedom. Freedom to do what I wanted and not find myself beholden to anyone or anything.

Right after the ESPN announcement, of course, my phone started blowing up—and it didn't stop ringing until much later that night. When things finally died down, I could relax.

This was it. My last day as a professional football player, and as I lay in bed that night, feeling good and happy and free, I was struck with another thought.

Now what?

CHAPTER 2

Beginnings

I was born on May 30, 1992, in Port Allen, Louisiana, a western suburb of Baton Rouge, the youngest of three children. My dad was Andre Sr., and my mom is Lisa. I have two older sisters, Tyquencia and Alancia. Ty is six years older than I am, and Lanci is two years older.

My childhood was pretty great. We weren't rich, but we did okay, and Port Allen is a small town where everybody knows everybody. That's how I grew up. My whole family pretty much lived there. I could walk from my house to one grandmother's house, then to my other grandmother's house, and there were always aunts and uncles and tons of cousins around. I have a lot of cousins. More than twenty. I often lose count of them, there are so many, but we all grew up tight, and everybody pretty much lives in either Baton

Rouge or Port Allen. Everywhere I ever needed to go, I could ride my bike.

Growing up with two older sisters, I found it easy to be the quiet one. I wasn't really pushed to the back as much as I *chose* to take the back seat a lot. I knew Ty and Lanci needed more attention than I did, and anyway, all I wanted to do was play. I just wanted to go outside and have fun. I was never the kind of kid who needed his mom to tell him to go outside and find something to do. I was just always on my own, always running around, playing, creating my own fun.

But it wasn't just about having fun. I always cleaned my room without anyone having to tell me. I always wanted to keep my stuff clean, always had good grades in school, never really got in trouble. Never, except this one time, when I stole a dollar from my mom to buy something from the ice cream truck, and when she realized what I did, she proceeded to whup my ass, and believe me, I never did it again.

My mother, Lisa West-Snearl, remembers the dollar-stealing incident a little differently. "First of all," she told me recently, "it was a hundred-dollar bill. You just thought you'd taken a dollar bill, and the ice cream man was kind enough to honk his horn, and I had to go out there. He said, 'I don't know if you meant to give him this amount of money,' and I had to tell him I didn't even know you were out there."

This is hilarious to me because I don't remember that part of it *at all*. I wasn't ever a bad kid, though I was a bit sneaky in an innocent way, such as sneaking outside to play even after I'd been told not to. I actually broke my arm once doing that. I was probably seven, and my mom had told me not to go skating outside because she had to go to work. I did it anyway and ended up falling and breaking my arm. She was understandably pissed off. It didn't help that Lanci was a bad influence, always pushing me to do that kind of thing. But more than anything else, my focus was on getting better at everything I did. Even as a kid, improving, growing, getting better at everything I did was always my first priority. I guess I was weird that way.

I don't remember my parents having too much trouble when I was really young, but I do remember them fighting more and more as I got to be seven or eight. I remember one time my mom ended up having to call the cops on my dad, and he actually put me in the truck with him when he left, saying, "I'll go, but I'm taking my son with me." That argument didn't last then, but eventually, things got worse.

It wasn't all the time, but every now and then they'd get into it. They would fuss about small things, like my dad staying out too late or sometimes not coming home at all. Finally, he was like, "You know what? I'm done with this." And he left.

My mom remembers me as a pretty good kid but with a lot to deal with. She said to me recently, "You were a happy kid. Any child that is not with both of their parents, I think that causes trauma. It was traumatizing because we started out as a married couple, and that's what you knew, but when your dad started getting on the drugs and being in and out, I had to shield you from that."

That part I do remember, her shielding me. I think I was about nine when he finally left. I can't remember the specific days, but I know he wasn't around much after that. He didn't move far away either, just to my grandmother's house. He was there if I needed him, and I could just walk over to see him, but that didn't happen very often. Now, if I had a game of some kind, basketball or football or a track meet, I could always count on him to show up for those, but otherwise? He was just sort of…absent, and it fell to my mom to be both parents for me.

My mom adds more clarity to what my childhood looked like, in her own words: "I don't think you ever knew this, but we were really poor. Pretty close to destitute. I worked very hard to protect you all from that and make you feel like we were doing okay, but we weren't. I saved up to make sure we could take a proper vacation every year, but to me, it was important that you had the things you needed."

This is just shocking to me. I had no idea until she told me as an adult that we were so poor. I think it's entirely possible that her drive to protect and take care of us was something that I picked up on and sunk in for me. My dad might have been a pretty bad influence, but my mother was a great one. I have long had a fear of ending up like my dad and have worked my butt off to avoid it. But the thing is, I think I just as badly wanted to end up like my mom. She was determined to make our lives better, working as hard as she could to do that for us. I looked up to her for that and wanted to emulate it.

One of the things I will keep coming back to throughout this book is the important lessons I've learned, why they're important, and how they might even be important to you in your own life. These are *life* lessons I want to share. Lessons that can translate to any person, from any background, in any line of work. An important lesson in this chapter is responsibility. Taking it, accepting it, owning it. My father never took responsibility for anything, and it showed. He displayed childish behavior until he died, something I'll talk about in great detail in the next chapter. But my mom was literally the opposite. She took responsibility and held on to it. She took care of us and shielded us, always putting my sisters and me ahead of herself.

As I got older and started to understand what responsibility was and what taking it and owning it meant, I ran toward it. If I made a mistake, I tried to admit it. If I was wrong, I tried to own up to it. If I upset someone, I tried to apologize for it. I keep saying "I tried" because, well, I'm not perfect, and I don't claim to be, so I'm sure there are times when I blew it. But what I learned at an early age, what my mom taught me, is that being able to admit you're wrong or when you screwed up and being able to apologize to someone when you've hurt them is a strength, not a weakness.

My father never did that. He never apologized. He never owned his mistakes. A lot of people think apologizing is a sign of weakness. That's just not true. It shows strength because it demonstrates that a person has enough confidence in themselves to admit when they're wrong. If a person insists they can't ever be wrong and they're not responsible for the things they say or do, what does that say about them? I'll tell you: It says that person is insecure. Irresponsible. Immature. Just like my dad.

After he died, my mom opened up to tell us more about the kind of man he was and why they ended up divorcing. She told us about how, when he was in the Army and they were stationed in Germany before I was born, he brought another woman to the house, saying it was his "friend." My mom actually cooked for her. She was young at the time and didn't really understand what was going on, but looking back on it, it's obvious that this was one of his girlfriends, right? She told us about him doing drugs, cheating—everything. When you're a kid, you don't think about that kind of stuff, you don't see it. You don't think about what kind of guy your dad is or whether you love him, you just do. Just like you love your mom. You don't want to see your parents fighting. But the truth of the matter is, my dad would never win any kind of best husband contest, that's for sure.

Years later, when I was in college, my mom got married again, this time to a great guy. But the marriage led to my dad breaking down and talking to me and Lanci about a lot of things he'd just never shared with us before. It was the first time in my life that he opened up to us, telling us how sorry he was about how he treated our mom and the way he treated us and how he wasn't around enough, all of that. I don't know if he was drunk or not—he was drunk a lot by then—but he started crying. I'd never seen him cry before. He was always a tough guy, but that night he apologized to us and said he wished he'd been a better father. It was the first time in my life that I saw him being truly vulnerable. I think it was the first time he ever apologized too. Honestly, it was surprising, and I didn't know how to react to it. Ultimately, I accepted his apology because I could see how sincere he was, but since I'd never seen him act like that before, I was confused.

I'll get much deeper into the complicated relationship I had with my father in the next chapter, but I'll scratch the surface here. There was clearly something in him that thought—maybe even hoped—that he and my mom weren't done. But when she married someone else and that door was closed to him forever, he reacted to it.

This was all just part of my reality as a kid. My sisters and I lived with my mom, and my dad lived a few blocks away. I saw him when I saw him, and that was it. But as I got older and it became clear that he would show up whenever I was playing sports, then that's what I did. I played as much sports as I could handle—not because I loved it but because I knew my dad would show up. It was a pretty simple equation for a kid: Playing sports equaled Dad showing up.

My first experience with organized sports happened when I was around six. My dad signed me up for soccer, and I was actually pretty good at it because I'm fast, and I could always beat everybody down the field and score all the goals. Then I got involved with track—again, because I was fast and because I knew my dad would come to see me play. I kept on with track all through high school, but as a little boy, just being able to run fast was great. This, apparently, was part of the plan. My mother knew, as things were starting to really fall apart at home, there was one sure way to keep me on the straight and narrow.

"I had two girls, and you were the only son," she told me. "And you were always busy with sports. It kept your mind occupied. You would leave early and come home late, and I just surrounded you with positive men, positive role models. Coaches and fathers who would come and pick you up."

Positive role models are important for all children but especially for young Black children who don't have strong father figures in their lives. This brings me to Eddie Payne, a local pastor we knew as simply "Mr. Eddie." He would pick up all the neighborhood kids who wanted to be picked up and take us to the track and train us for free. We'd play basketball with him, we'd play softball with him, we'd play volleyball, on and on, but track was the main thing. After he picked us up around six in the morning, we'd go to church, we'd pray and sing, and then we'd go to the school, where they'd serve breakfast to the neighborhood kids during summertime. After that, we'd finally go to the track and run, which is really how I got into sports.

There were a lot of us, in fact, who got into sports solely because of Mr. Eddie. Probably twenty kids would pile into Mr. Eddie's big red-and-white van every day. He'd blow the horn in the morning, and we'd get up and go, eager to play whatever sport he had planned for us that day; then he'd bring us home around two o'clock, after lunch. That was my first experience of being on a team. Mr. Eddie created that kind of collective, close-knit atmosphere in our community, and some of the best friends I have—friends that I still have to this day—I met because of Mr. Eddie. There's a street named after him now in Port Allen. That's how influential he is there. That's the man who got me into sports.

"He got you into sports," my mom said, "because, as a young Black man, I knew I had to get you out of that environment, and I wanted you around fathers, coaches, men who were positive and responsible and would be a good influence. You didn't know I was doing it, but that was my purpose. Your dad wasn't there, and I didn't want you just staying in the house, bickering with me and two girls."

As usual, my mom's protective instincts had a positive impact on my life from the very beginning. But it was more than instincts, it was *love*. Mom did everything she could to make my life more fun and more enjoyable, even as hers was falling apart. And she was right about how those men influenced me. There's no doubt that they were the positive role models that I never really had in my own dad.

She was also right about me and sports. I loved sports, was good at them, and spent all my time playing them. Track was helpful to me because of the mental aspect. Knowing that I was good and that I was fast enough to beat anybody kind of built me up and gave me confidence. I think it also made me more of a competitor, because I was part of a team, but I also ran for myself. When you're in the starting blocks, it's scary because you're by yourself with nobody around. It's you against everyone else.

That taught me another lesson I carried with me. A wrong lesson, actually, and one that would, in time, end up repeatedly working against me. But that's the thing about lessons: even if you learn a lesson that's difficult or wrong, it can still be valuable if you also learn to distinguish the *difference*.

For a while, I was convinced that the only person really looking out for me was me. Obviously, my mom was on my side, and so was my family, but in my mind I couldn't talk to other people about stuff that was bothering me. They'd either think I was weak or they wouldn't understand. I tricked myself into thinking I could work everything out for myself. This is ridiculous, of course, but that's how I felt at the time. If something bothered me as a teen, I'd hold on to it. I'd never deal with it or discuss it in any kind of healthy way. This carried through to college and beyond, and I will talk about the specifics of that in due time, but it was a bad lesson.

Eventually, the right lesson surfaced. From wrong can come right, and in this case, here's the lesson that matters most: It is always, *always* better to talk to someone when something is bothering you. Try not to hold it in. Share it with someone. Try to understand that this is not a sign of weakness but a sign of strength, in the same way that being able to apologize and own up to your mistakes is a sign of strength. Again, this requires a shift in mindset.

We'll be coming back to that plenty because we're going to come to several different points in my life where I needed to learn that lesson again, but for now, I'm eight years old, and my dad has decided to sign me up for football. My mom, though, was not happy about it at first because she thought I was too small. I was always small. Always. Even when I grew up and went to the NFL, I was considered small. Coaches mentioned it, recruiters were concerned about it, and my opponents underestimated me because of it. I topped out at five-foot-ten, which is an average size for a regular person but, let's face it, small for a professional football player. I didn't reach my full height until I was about sixteen or seventeen. But when I was eight, when I first started playing football, I was downright tiny. People always told me I couldn't do this or that because of my small size, but to my dad's credit, when it came to that, he was always in my corner.

Mom was supportive, but she was also scared. That's part of being a mom, right? No mother wants to see their child get hurt. She didn't think it was a good idea for me to play football, but my dad just kind of overruled her. I kept playing and never stopped.

My mom is still very clear about why she was so concerned: "You were so skinny," she said. "Your dad was like that too, but I was trying to talk you into more track and basketball because football was such a tough sport. And for a mom, people think we're on the sideline cheering, but a real mom is *praying*. We're really just counting down the seconds till the game is over, we're praying for those four quarters to come to an end, for that moment your child walks away with every bone in his body together. It did work out well for you in the end, of course."

It sure did. My first team was the Baton Rouge Rams, one of the best youth football teams in Baton Rouge at the time. A lot of my track guys played for the same team, so I wanted to play with them. And, like I said, my dad was always there. I knew right away that if I played football, my dad was going to be there, so I just said, "Yeah, I've got to play football."

My dad didn't just come to the games, he came to the practices too, and he would really get into it. One practice, I'll never forget this, I was playing receiver. I played both sides of the ball, defensive back, of course, and also usually quarterback. But this time I was playing receiver, and I ran a slant route. So I'm running the route, the ball comes to me, and I drop it. My dad came off the sidelines and said, "No, run the play again." This time he goes out to play linebacker during the play.

So I'm running the play again. They snap the ball, I run across the middle of the field, the ball comes at me, and my dad lights. Me. Up. I mean, he *clobbered* me. The ball is flying in the air, and all I see is my feet as I tumble head over heels.

He just knocked me on my butt, and as I was lying there, out of breath, he said, "Yeah, you'll never drop the ball again."

And I didn't. Not once did I ever drop the ball again after that day. He hit me so hard, I'm like, "What the hell? Why would you come on the field and do this?" But I understand it now: He was just trying to make me better. In his mind, he was making sure I never forgot that hit. It obviously worked.

The funny thing is, the coaches didn't say anything when it happened. Nobody said a word. Everyone got up and went back to the huddle. Of course, back then, football was all about toughness. About winning. They didn't care about the other stuff, and no one knew that getting hit in the head like that was bad for you. In fact, from the coaches' perspective, that was an excellent lesson. Sometimes you're going to get hit in the head, and you just gotta get back up and keep going.

I played three seasons with the Rams, from when I was eight to when I was ten. Then I went back to Port Allen and played for the Port Allen Ambassadors. My uncle was actually my coach then, my mom's sister's husband. I played quarterback for him for two years. Usually I just ran the ball because I was so much faster than everyone else, but I did throw it now and again—and cornerback, sometimes safety, when the other team had two good receivers.

What was it I liked so much about football? Besides the fact that I knew it meant my father would show up? I also just loved competing, man. And I liked being on the field. Obviously, seeing my dad was a big part of that, but just being on the field was the key. The only time he ever missed a game was when he was in jail for a DUI, and he was gone for six months, but otherwise, he never missed one. It's funny, actually, one time we were playing while he was in jail, and I hit a guy so hard *my* nose started bleeding. I called my dad in jail to tell him about it. We had a good laugh. It's odd now, thinking about moments like these as good times, but they were.

Once he was out of the state penitentiary, he was back for every game. Every football game, basketball game, track meet. He was there.

So basically my dad's love of football translated to me. And the fact that I was able to bond with him over football is part of what made me love it. Or, at least, what made me *think* that I loved it. It wasn't necessarily the contact or anything like that, because as I mentioned before, I never really liked getting hit. It was just my dad. It made me want to be better because he loved watching football. Maybe if he'd been a big baseball fan, I might have pursued that. We'll never know.

I missed one year of football when I was thirteen because I was too old for the peewee league and my middle school didn't have a team. My mom put me in a magnet school in Baton Rouge, which was good for my grades and because I was smart, but it wasn't big on sports. She wanted me to be academically challenged, which I was, but then I returned to Port Allen for high school because I wanted to play with my friends. But my time playing high school football is a different chapter, so we'll get to that.

There are some other important lessons I learned playing football as a kid. One was that hard work gets you a long way. To be successful in anything, a great work ethic is required. (Again, this goes beyond football.) Since I was always the smallest kid on the field, or one of the smallest, I had to work harder than everyone else. That made me one of the best players too. A bigger kid would see me on the field and he'd smile, and then I would knock him on his butt. I wasn't afraid to tackle anybody. It wasn't the contact that mattered, and my being able to make this contact with other players who were usually bigger than me showed that you couldn't mess with me. If you were a receiver, and I had you as a cover corner, I'd let you know it was coming. In the seventh grade, I warned a kid that if he came around the end and didn't see me, I would knock him off his block. And I did. Often.

I totally had the small-man syndrome, going on the attack so people didn't try to take advantage of me. I didn't care how big you were, it just made me want to come out even stronger. I wanted to show you I was better than you.

That translated to other things too. Being disciplined, being able to focus, it all came from hard work, and I understood that no matter what people told me, if I just kept working, I would get better eventually, and that's what happened. I kept working—on the football field, on the track, wherever I was—and I *kept getting better*. The lesson here is this: Have a strong work ethic. If you don't have one, create one. I can't say it enough. It's one of the most important steps to take on the path to success.

This lesson extends far beyond the football field. This extends to life in general: if you've got the drive, if you're willing to work for what you want and force yourself to get better at it, you will get the job done. I'm not going to offer up any empty clichés here—nothing about the size of the dog in the fight or anything like that—I'll just give it to you straight: hard work, determination, believing in yourself, pushing yourself toward constant improvement, all of these will carry you to the end zone. They certainly did for me.

This reminds me of a famous quote by Jim Rohn, a businessman, author, and motivational speaker, who said, "We must all suffer from one of two pains: the pain of discipline or the pain of regret. The difference is discipline weighs ounces while regret weighs tons." That says everything.

It was around this time when I was about twelve or thirteen that I started taking better care of my body too. That was a big transition for me, doing pushups and sit-ups and paying attention to how I exercised and how I treated my body. I started watching a lot more football and decided I wanted to play pro ball, and my sister Ty told me that if I wanted to get better and have a better shot, then I needed to get bigger. Then my dad suggested the pushups and sit-ups, which I started doing every night.

I started paying a lot more attention to the nuances of the game, too, and began to realize how important it was for me to understand it on a deeper level. I looked at the players and started thinking about their physicality as well. How big do you have to be to play this position or to play that position? If I want to be a running back, what do I need to get up to the optimal size? Would being a defensive back maybe be a better fit? What position can I play best? Where can I be successful? Those were the questions I was constantly thinking about. Always evaluating, always teaching myself how to analyze situations and see how they would affect me, and it was incredibly valuable, off the field as well as on. It was something I learned at a young age, figuring out exactly where you are and how you're thinking. How you can optimize your situation by asking yourself tough questions.

I also started paying a lot more attention to what I ate. As a kid, I never ate much; sometimes I had to remind myself to do it. But then when I realized how important nutrition was and how I would need to practice better nutrition to get bigger, I focused on it, even if I still didn't care all that much about *eating*. Honestly, I knew that it would help me, so I was just doing it because I wanted to get bigger. My dad was good about that kind of thing, and my attitude was, if my dad says it, I'll do it.

The thing is, when you're eight, nine, ten years old, and you're suddenly doing pushups and sit-ups every night, and you're paying more attention to what you're eating and when you're eating it, and realizing there are a lot of things I have to do if I want to be bigger, if I want to have more fun and more success playing this game, what you're really doing is *laying the groundwork for taking better care of yourself*. It's establishing a pattern for the rest of your life. Even if you don't realize it when you're that young, you pick up on it as you get a little older. When you're twenty years old, you're allowing your ten-year-old self to take care of you. And when you're thirty years old, you're allowing your twenty-year-old self to take care of you. You can always make up for it later by changing your habits, but half the battle is developing good habits in the first place. I realize that now, even if I had no idea about it then.

There was one more incredibly important lesson I learned when I was a kid, a lesson that also came directly from my dad. Whatever his faults were, and he had plenty, he had an enormous amount of faith in me. He knew before I did that I was actually pretty good at sports. Knowing he had that much confidence in me made me realize that I was good enough. And he always told me, until the day he died, "The cream will always rise to the top." He said it to me when I was just a kid, "The cream rises." I'd be upset after a game that maybe the ball didn't come to me enough or I didn't get enough to do, and I'd say, "Man, they aren't giving me the ball," and he would just tell me, "The cream will rise to the top." Even when I went to the NFL and I was a rookie who wasn't playing much, he would repeat it. "The cream rises to the top. The cream rises to the top." Meaning, the best stuff will always come out ahead in the end.

Sure enough, the next year I'm a starter, and I lead the Texans in interceptions. Faith is a big deal, and showing it in others goes a long way. Especially when they really need to hear it. If you tell someone over and over again how great they are, eventually they're going to believe it. It sure did with me and my dad. From an athletic perspective, he always had the most faith in me, oftentimes more than I had in myself. I think that his confidence in me probably gave me the extra push I needed to make it because he made it clear that it didn't matter how big or small you are. You're either good enough to do what you want to do, or you're not, and I was. This was instilled in me at a very young age. He made me know, made me understand, that I was good enough. That I could do this. Here's another important lesson: *self-confidence is a mindset.* And over time, you can strengthen this mindset, this way of thinking, if you really make the effort.

It's ironic, in a way, the fact that my dad was able to instill so much self-confidence in me even though he was rarely around. If I needed him, I could find him, but I never needed him in that way. I just knew he'd be there when I played the next game, you know? Knowing he was there when I played was important, even if I never really needed him the rest of the time. As an adult, I've had conversations with people about what it was like growing up, and what I've realized is that each of us only knows our own experience.

For me, not having my dad around was natural. It was just the way it was. I wouldn't beat myself up about it or even feel sad about it and think, "Ah, my dad was never around," I just thought that was what dads *did*, and I'd see him when I saw him. When I had a football game, he was there, so it makes sense that I dove into football. He probably wouldn't show up for dinner at night, but if I was playing in a game, I knew he'd show up for that. So I had to keep playing.

Like I said, my relationship with my dad was complicated. So go ahead and turn the page, and we'll get into it.

CHAPTER 3

Endings (and New Beginnings)

So let's talk about my dad. Andre Hal Sr. was born in Port Allen, Louisiana, on January 18, 1964. He died there on October 16, 2018, at the age of fifty-four. In between, he was married and divorced, fathered three children, and his only son played in the NFL, which is something not a lot of people can say. He took terrible care of himself, drank too much, did too many drugs, was a lousy husband and could've been a much better father, and ultimately died of congestive heart failure four days after he had a massive heart attack.

But that's the easy stuff. The surface-level stuff. The stuff everyone knows. Obviously, he was a whole lot more than that. He was also the life of the party, the guy who would get it started. He was athletic. When I was a kid, he would race me and beat me. I was crazy fast, but until I was thirteen, he could always beat me in a foot race. That's how athletic he was. We played basketball together. He just loved sports. If there was one thing that he was really into, that was it. All he wanted to do was watch football, basketball, baseball—anything on ESPN.

But as I've already mentioned, he was not very mature for his age. He kind of just lived his life the way he wanted and never really took on many responsibilities. I also feel like his mother, my grandmother, babied him. She enabled him to do a lot of things he shouldn't have done. It's a long list. One thing on that list: leaving my mom and going to live with my grandma, who just let him stay there. Another thing on the list (before he and my mom broke up): leaving the house and staying away for three or four days at a time. Or never helping my mom with child support. Or giving him chance after chance, even though he kept screwing up, getting drunk, and coming home high. I just never liked that a mother—his mother—would let a son do that to his family. He didn't take his responsibilities seriously enough, I guess, because my grandma enabled him to just be a kid all his life. She pampered and spoiled him. It showed even more when he got older.

Once he got married and had kids, you could tell he never really matured. It wasn't obvious to me as a kid, of course, but as I got older, I started realizing that my dad never really grew up. Never matured. Fortunately, though, I did. I left to go to college, and I worked hard to make sure I made good grades and stayed in school, and I developed that same focus on the football field too. But while I was doing this, while I was working my butt off to succeed and to move forward, it finally dawned on me that my dad had been sitting in neutral (or worse, moving in reverse) and doing the same useless thing all my life. Just kicking it. It occurred to me that I'd never seen him work hard for anything. Suddenly, I had all these responsibilities, all these commitments...and my dad was just *chilling*.

You know, it's a weird dynamic to see as a kid growing up that your dad is still kind of in the kid stage while you're developing into a man. But it's just how he was. I don't know if it was his fault or if it was my grandmother's fault or maybe the fault belonged to both of them, but whatever the case, he refused to grow up. Like Peter Pan but in real life. Seeing this right in front of me, throughout my whole life, helped me realize that I didn't want to be like my dad. That's why I always pushed myself to be better. It made me want to work harder. Here's another important lesson: knowing what you *don't* want to be sometimes helps you decide what you do want to be.

On the one hand, I wanted his approval, but on the other, I didn't want to *be like* him. It felt like a strange balance, but that's just the way it was, and I dealt with it the best way I knew how. Looking back on it, I realize I didn't really understand my dad until I got older. It wasn't until I went off to college that I started to realize that he was not the man that maybe I thought he was. Before that, even for all his faults, I still saw him as a father figure. But then again, I didn't know any different. We only know what we live, right?

My dad never really disciplined me in high school, and like I've said before, he wasn't really there for me unless I had a football game or a track meet, but I still had the respect for him that a son would have for his father. I didn't fully understand everything that was really going on. That he was living with his mom. That he wasn't paying bills. I didn't understand what a man was supposed to do because I had no other frame of reference, nothing else to compare it to. Not until I got to college and started seeing other guys' fathers come to the stadium or come to the dorm room or really sit down and just talk to them, give them good advice, did I realize this was how dads were supposed to act with their children. It was then that it hit me with full force: my dad was more of a buddy than a father. Which is how I started treating him from that moment forward for the rest of his life.

Through it all, though, my mom never talked badly about him because she didn't want me to hate him. When I recently asked her why she was so good to him on my behalf, especially after he'd been so bad to her, she said, "You know that I am a very spiritual, God-fearing person. I'm a Christian, and I base everything on the word of God, and I knew that if I ran my house as a single parent, as a spiritual person, that you kids would be okay, and I knew that saying bad things about your father would not help you at all."

Which pretty much tells you everything you need to know about how special my mom is. She was so tough and so strong that I learned more about being a man from her than from anyone else. She made sure I wasn't just sitting on my butt, and I did *everything*. I washed the dishes. I cooked. I cleaned. I cut the grass. I did every chore, and today I know how to do things. And I know how to treat women, too—with the respect, dignity, and love they deserve. She taught me that. She helped me transition from the little boy that I was then to the man that I am today. That's the thing about transitions: Other people can help guide you along the way. You don't have to do it all by yourself. You can let others help you. I'm thankful that my mom taught me all these important lessons. And I'm grateful I can share some of these lessons with you now.

But back to my dad. The little things I mentioned before, like never coming to visit me in school, they added up, and that's when I realized it was all just about football. All about my athletic ability. That was why he came around all the time, and maybe if I hadn't been such a great athlete, he'd never have come around at all. I suddenly got it in a way I never had before. As a kid, I just thought that's how life is. Mom's around all the time, but Dad only comes around for a football game. Okay. It never dawned on me that he was supposed to be around all the time too.

When he was around, though, he did care. I don't want to make it seem like he didn't because my success clearly was very important to him. He didn't give me the normal kind of father-son guidance—we never really talked about sex or anything like that unless we were joking about it—but he did give me plenty of advice on how to get better athletically. Like, "Do the pushups every night, do the sit-ups every night." Stuff like that, to get my body right. But mentally, he didn't really give me much to fulfill me or to help me grow into being a man, other than pushing me to be tough and demanding and to go on the field knowing that I was good enough to play the game. He gave me the confidence that he believed in me more than I believed in myself, which is a lot, but as I was developing as a man and growing up, he gave me very little.

Most of who I am now—knowing how to act, how to treat people, how to behave—I get from my mom. The conversation I mentioned last chapter, after my mom got remarried, was the first real conversation my dad and I ever had because in every other one throughout my entire life, we were either joking around or we were talking about sports. Never once did I have a real, sit-down, man-to-man conversation with him, and I think a big part of that was that I don't believe he *knew* how to have it. It just wasn't in him. And then I went off to college and started distancing myself more and more from him. Most of all I didn't want to be like him, and the easiest way for me to do that was to not be around him. I'd check in now and then, say hi, but otherwise I kept him at arm's length.

There was even one time when he came to a game, and afterward he asked me for money. He's asking me, a college kid, for money! I had to say, "Come on, man, I'm struggling too." I think that was when I started to actively push him away. I realized that he just wasn't doing much, and I'm out here, working my butt off, and you're going to ask me for money? Come on.

The good thing about this is that someday I'd like to have kids of my own, and when that happens, I'll know what *not* to do. I want to be able to sit down with them and have real conversations with them, teach them stuff, and do the things my dad never did. That's my goal, at least.

After I graduated from Vanderbilt and was drafted by the Houston Texans, my dad started coming to me asking for all kinds of stuff. He felt like he deserved what he was asking of me, but I had to nip that in the bud real quick. That's when I sat him down and had my first real adult conversation with him, telling him, "I can't give you the things you're demanding because you weren't really there. How do you expect me to just give, give, give, when you weren't around?"

He was angry, and we didn't talk for a couple of weeks after that, but then he eventually came to his senses and lowered his expectations. Not too long after that, though, he asked me to buy him a truck. I resisted at first, but he kept coming and kept coming, and finally I said okay, and gave him a little cash for a car. A piece of junk I picked up for a couple thousand dollars. I think he had it a couple of months, and I don't even know what happened to it, but it was all I could give him. I couldn't give that much to my mom, and he expected more. Crazy.

He wanted money, he wanted help, he wanted all kinds of things. I offered him game tickets. Eventually, after I kept saying no to his other requests, he realized that the tickets were all he was going to get. I talked about my work ethic and how it made me who I am today. Well, my dad's *lack* of work ethic made him who he was. He was a good athlete in high school but then got into some trouble and went into the Army. When he got out, he did as little as possible, taking home some money from his military pension, but when he needed quick cash, he'd do a little work for my uncle, who has a concrete business. He'd pour concrete, make some quick cash, and then go back to drinking and smoking and hanging out, doing nothing.

But I don't want to make it seem like it was all bad because it wasn't. We did have some fun, and later, when his health started to fail, we had a few conversations that went beyond the superficial stuff that we'd always covered. I'll get to that in a bit, but the most important thing here is to reiterate just how important he was to my football career. And to instilling in me a sense of self-confidence.

There are a couple of ways to look at this. One is that his absence made my life, and the lives of my mom and my sisters, more challenging and that he was a terrible role model for me. That, if not for my mom's guidance and my own desire to be the best, could have led me down a very dark path.

But I choose to look at it another way: that his presence at my athletic events gave those games and meets and competitions even more meaning. I associated them with his love, which gave them more power. Football didn't mean that much to me, but thinking that success in football would lead to more love from my dad? That absolutely did. Combine that with the tangible benefit he brought to my life—instilling in me the bulletproof belief that I was good enough to do anything—and he deserves at least some of the credit for my success. Not as much as I do, or my mom does, and not enough for me to buy him anything he wanted, but some, for sure.

This was never clearer to me than when he started to fall apart in the months leading up to his death. At some point, he realized that his health was declining, and that's when he at least tried to change. We noticed a difference in him. I could tell he was trying. He would call me sometimes and want to talk about things other than football. It surprised me, and I was often like, "What?" But I could tell he was trying, y'know? He'd ask how I was doing or how practice was or how I was doing with my girlfriend, things he'd never really bothered with before.

I remember thinking to myself, "Okay, you want to talk to me about this? I'm down. Let's *talk*." Especially since he was clearly making an effort. I even started asking him about his own childhood, and he told me he wasn't too close with his dad either. He was trying to get more out of me, I think, but I kept brushing it off. It changed a little, though, when I realized that he was trying to get his life back on track. One day before we got off the phone, he even said, "I love you." I said, "I love you, too," but thought it was odd that he would say it. It was probably the first time he'd ever told me he loved me, so of course I hadn't expected it. It didn't hit me until a while after I was off the phone with him that he'd said, "I love you." I wasn't used to that, so I didn't really know what to do with it. I think he knew. He knew he had heart trouble and didn't tell anyone.

Then, on Friday, October 12, 2018, he had the heart attack that would eventually kill him. We had no idea how bad it was at first. I got the call and thought, "Okay, that's Dad, he'll bounce back. He always bounces back." I'd never had anything this bad happen, so it didn't make sense to me that he might actually *die*. I just thought, "He'll be okay, he's just in the hospital." At first, they didn't tell me any details, that he was unconscious in a coma, so I thought he was just lying in a hospital, chillin'. He'd be there for a couple days and then be out. I wasn't even planning on coming home because there was a game that Sunday. I had been out for the first few games of the season and was going to play soon, but the team still needed me to wear a headset in the game and help the defense from the sidelines, so I was getting ready for that.

But then, the next day, Saturday, my grandmother called and told me, "You might need to come up here because he's not looking too good." That's when I started to wonder what was really going on, so I hopped in my car and drove up, got there late, like nine or ten o'clock that night, and first thing Sunday morning we headed over to the hospital. He was still out. He was on the ventilator, and his hands were still moving a bit, but the doctor wasn't sure what was going to happen and said they wanted to see if he would wake up by himself. I'd certainly never seen him in that kind of predicament. He'd always been up and around and doing stuff, so seeing him down like that was very jarring.

I had to head back to Houston for the game, so I left. As I said, I was still inactive and worked the headset for the defense, but then, right after the game, I turned around and drove back to Port Allen to be with my dad. Sunday night, all day Monday, he wasn't waking up on his own, his blood pressure kept dropping, and we started asking what was really going on.

The doctor came in and told us it wasn't looking too good, and he asked us to start thinking about what we wanted to do. Did we want to keep him alive on a ventilator and pray for a miracle? Or did we want to let him go? Ty said that she didn't want to see our dad live like that, as a vegetable, which is what he'd become. But my grandmother had already lost her two other sons (one died of AIDS before I was born and the other had died the year earlier of complications from diabetes), so my dad was the last surviving one, and she didn't want to let him go.

This led to a huge fight between my sister and my grand-mother. My sister was saying, "He's just a body, he's not really here anymore. We can't talk to him, he can't understand us, so why keep him on machines?" Meanwhile, my grandma was saying, "No! We *got* to keep him alive! We *got* to keep him alive!"

It got really heated, and in the middle of it, something occurred to me—this single thought came to my mind: "If we keep him alive, it's only his body that's still going, not his mind." Whatever made him the person he was? That was gone, and the only reason we might continue to keep him around was for us, to give us some solace, not for him. He got no benefit from it. To keep him alive, I thought, was selfish.

So when someone in the room said that this wasn't something we needed to decide right then, I spoke up and said, "Oh, yes it is. We're deciding this now."

That's when something really strange happened and is part of why I am a spiritual person. I think my dad's spirit was there. He felt the tension of the situation, the high emotions in the room, and he simply decided to move on. All of a sudden, his blood pressure dropped like a stone, going down lower and lower, and then the heart monitor started beeping and going crazy. Just like that, right in front of us, my father was gone. He'd made the decision for us. He left. Then the room got really quiet. The doctors came in and tried to revive him, but he was gone. I felt a sense of loss, and I was sad but not as sad as I thought I would be. Strangely, I felt good that he wasn't in pain anymore.

That was Tuesday, October 16. That morning, before this all happened, the general manager had called to tell me the team had activated me and that I was going to play my first game of the season the following Sunday. Immediately, I thought, "Well, this is going to be the craziest week ever."

It's all still a bit of a blur, but I played, hurt my shoulder, went to the postgame press conference and answered questions about what it was like to be back, and never even mentioned to anyone that my dad had just died five days earlier. Not to anyone. Not to my coaches, not to my teammates, not to the press, *nobody*. I just didn't want to deal with all the stuff that would go along with having it out there, people asking, "Are you sure you want to play?" and other questions like that. Yes. I wanted to play. If I didn't want to, I wouldn't have, so why bother talking about it? I also knew that if I was focused on getting back on the field, it would help me with the internal stuff about my dad dying. Our relationship was based on sports, and he was around when I was playing but not the rest of the time when I needed him. Now I was playing, and he wasn't there, and I had to deal with how to do that without him.

I compartmentalized my dad's death, plain and simple. Tucked it away neatly in the back corner of my mind where I didn't really have to think about it all that much. Truth be told, I was just happy to be back out on the field.

Eventually, I told people about my dad's death, and of course they asked me how I was able to play, but I just said I was playing for him, basically. I wanted back on the field for him, but I realized I wanted it for myself, too. There were a lot of reasons to get back on the field, and one of them was to see how I felt without him watching.

Immediately, I knew something was off. After that first game, I remember thinking to myself, "Damn, I don't have to play for you anymore, Dad." I didn't wrap my head around it that quickly, but I knew something was off. The adrenaline that had been pumping through my body all that week had worn off, and I knew something wasn't right—I just wasn't sure yet what it was. It would take me almost six months to get to that final decision about retirement, as you know, but at that moment, it was just a feeling that something was *missing*. Something felt off-balance. When it came time for the next game, I didn't feel the same way I usually did before a game. I couldn't get hyped enough for it, couldn't get myself as pumped up as I had in the past. It used to be easy. Now it was suddenly very hard. Something was definitely off.

I'd had serious health issues, I'd come back to football, I should have been great. I should have been excited. The team was good, we were headed for the playoffs, I was playing well, so it all should have added up to something really good, but instead it just felt *empty*. I tried to make everything feel normal, but normal was gone. And because my dad was dead, I knew "normal" wasn't coming back.

For a while, I thought it was just because I was in mourning. With that in mind, I threw myself even more into the game, which was something I already played at a high level, but I went at it even more, and I did great. I had three interceptions in six games, which tied me for the team lead for the whole season. I was having a great year, even though I missed half of it.

I was all over the place. I had to focus on playing football to keep me centered, but at the same time, football didn't give me that anymore. I didn't want people to feel sorry for me, but in doing that, I was working hard to please others rather than taking care of myself. Looking back, I think I was really damaging both my mental and physical selves by not facing what was really hurting me. Not dealing with the real problem. Trying to be "the man," which meant being tough, not showing emotions or vulnerability, refusing to crack, staying strong, just shutting up and playing good football—because that's who I am.

At least, that's who I *thought* I was. It's all the standard garbage we're supposed to believe is what makes you a man, even though it's not. Not at all. I was in pain but couldn't bring myself to talk to anyone about it. I didn't know how. I just tried to figure out on my own what was going on in my head instead of reaching out to somebody because I felt like nobody would understand anyway.

In retrospect, this was stupid because it was a lesson I'd already learned my freshman year of college during a crisis of a different sort. I'll get to that soon enough, but the lesson I'd learned then, and which I was not enacting now, is that *it's always better to talk to someone* and that turning to someone for help (or talking to someone just so they can listen) is not a sign of weakness but a sign of strength. Being a man is not about restraining emotions or refusing to show vulnerability. It's just the opposite. Being a man means being strong enough, confident enough, and wise enough to express your emotions and to turn to those you trust when you feel like you need to. Simple as that.

My whole life I had poured everything I had into football to bring myself closer to my father. Now my father was gone, so what did football hold for me anymore? That was my dilemma, and no matter how much I thought about it, I couldn't find a good answer.

What I ended up doing was just keeping to myself and trying to work through it all by myself. This took a while— probably a lot longer than if I'd talked to someone about it— and a lot of developing on my part, but it made me a different person. I had to change myself to kind of figure out what was going on. Because of the work I'd been doing, I was able to internalize things better, to work through them in a way I hadn't been able to do before. I had a better understanding about life because I thought more about it.

We made it through the season, were the number three seed in the AFC, and hosted a playoff game against the sixth-seed Indianapolis Colts on January 5, 2019. It was a game we were favored to win, but we lost 21-7 and were eliminated.

The days and weeks leading up to the end of the season and to that game, I stayed as present as I could be, but the truth is, when the end came, it was a huge relief. In the fourth quarter, as it became clear we weren't going to come back and pull it out, it was an enormous weight off my shoulders. As the clock ticked down, I realized how tired I was.

The last couple months had been so stressful, and I'd fractured my shoulder and played through it, so I was in physical pain too. But this was my job. They're paying me to play, and play well, and while the season is going, I'm going to put the job first and me second. But once the season was over, I knew I'd be able to just focus on myself, focus on Dre.

That's what I thought as the game ended. It would've been great to win the game, and then the next one, and the next one, and go to the Super Bowl, but I was just so tired. The year had been such a long, difficult one, and now it was over.

Walking off the field, I thought to myself, "Okay, now it's Dre Time. Time to sit down and figure out where my head is, what I want, and what I need."

So that's what I did.

CHAPTER 4

High School Star

I should just say right off the bat that I was on the varsity football team all four years of high school. I also played JV my freshman year, so I'd play JV Wednesday night, then varsity Friday night, which sounds like a lot, but when you're fourteen, it's not a big deal. Nobody else seemed to think it was a big deal either, and I guess I didn't care. Junior varsity was easy.

I didn't start on the varsity team until about the sixth game of the season, but once I did, I started every other game I played through my senior year, and after that first year, I played both sides of the ball, offense and defense. Cornerback on defense, receiver on offense, and I also returned punts and kicks, so the only time I wasn't on the field was when we were punting. Otherwise, I was out there.

After my peewee football career, people knew who I was, especially the coaches at Port Allen, who wanted me to come to school and play there. My old track coach, he coached at the high school at the time, and he was telling my mom, "Make sure your son comes to my school." He wanted me to go to school with his son, who was also there, and we'd been running track together for years. We wanted to build something for the coach at Port Allen High. A bunch of my other friends were going there, so we decided to all go together and try to change the culture there.

Even though I didn't start right away, I felt I deserved to. The coaches thought I wasn't ready yet, but around the sixth game of the season, there were a couple of injuries, and they put me in the starting lineup. It was against Clinton High in October 2006, and they happened to have one of the best receivers in the state, a guy named Luther Loyell. I'll never forget that first game.

It's my first game as a starting corner, and I'm against a total star. I'm still small too. I was about five-feet-seven or eight by then, but I was still really, really skinny. Like, 130 pounds. Tiny.

So, anyway, I'm covering Loyell one-on-one, and he is just *killing* me. I think he scored three times out, and one of the seniors started yelling at the coaches, "Get that freshman out of the game!" I mean, I was just getting lit up, and he kept beating me over and over. Lots of catches, lots of yards, and after the game, I said to myself, "I will never get killed like that in a game again." Right then and there I made that pledge.

I talked to my old high school coach Guy Blanchard, and he still remembers that game, too. He said, "That first game, in all fairness to you, I wanted to start you out of the box and let you learn on the field. My philosophy was, the only way to be ready is to get ready. That first game you had a rough night, and I remember after that telling you, 'Hey, man, welcome to the big leagues.' Then you knew where you had to go.

"We knew early on that you were gonna be a great player," he continued, "but as a true freshman, there were some plays you got beat on, and there was talk that if an older guy was in that spot, it would've been different, but I knew you were special, that you were gonna be great."

Remember all that confidence my dad helped instill in me? It was that very confidence that kept me together after that game. When I swore I'd never get beat like that again, I knew I never would, and I never did. Maybe some guys would've been broken by that game, would've believed maybe they weren't as good as they thought they were, getting so beat up like that. But for me, like Coach said, it was just, "Welcome to the big leagues." I knew it could only get better from there. That's another important lesson: You can learn to let the not-so-great things that happen to you in life motivate you, spur you, inspire you to do better. From bad can definitely come good. You can move from *bad* to *better* to *best*.

That summer, I dedicated my life to getting bigger and stronger and in better shape. I kept thinking about that first game, the night when Loyell was really toasting me, and my teammate was yelling at my coach to, "Get that freshman out of the game." I was obsessed with never letting something like that happen again, and I worked my butt off the whole summer to get better.

The rest of my freshman year, I played basketball in the winter and ran track in the spring. I played basketball my first two years, then decided to drop it junior year, so instead I ran indoor track. Basketball was always fun, and I was really good on defense. I was so fast, I could lock down the other team's best players, and I could really jump, even if I wasn't that tall and was still so skinny. By sophomore year, I could dunk. I never really scored all that much, but I didn't care about that. It was more fun to me to keep the other guy from scoring, and I would usually use up all five fouls doing it. After sophomore year, though, I knew that I wasn't going to get to the next level playing basketball. I realized that football was my ticket, and I didn't want to take the risk of getting hurt playing hoops, so I gave it up.

But that summer after freshman year, once I was done running track, I went to a trainer named Reggie Williams, and he became my mentor. I still talk to him today. One of the best guys I've ever met. His son and daughter both ran track, too. That's how we all knew each other. He mostly trained college players, anybody who was training to go into the NFL, or kids like me who were planning to go to college. Everybody trained with Reggie. I would go work out with my team in the morning, then train with Reggie in the afternoons, so I was doing two-a-days five days a week. With Reggie, it was quickness drills, strength drills, running through defensive backfield drills, all that stuff. And I'd also run the levee.

Oh man, the levee. And yes, I mean a *real* levee—the embankment that holds back the overflow of a river. I'd do drills on that levee. That thing's steep, and we'd run it over and over again. Running up, then backpedaling down. Up and down, up and down. The levee actually would make you faster, you know, going up that incline, building your leg strength, your quads and calves, your endurance; it helps with everything, and that was Reggie's signature thing. "You gotta go run the levee," he'd always say, or, "Hey! Go run the levee!" I absolutely believe that was one of the tools that made me a better athlete. It helped me get to the next level.

When I came back for my sophomore year, I was faster, stronger, quicker. I was the starting cornerback, and I was locking stuff down. I never had to go up against another guy like Luther Loyell—because you don't go up against guys like that too often, the best in the state—but that didn't matter. I was getting better and better, and I had this driving belief inside me that nobody was going to beat me. Not ever. I was working on my DB skills so that it wouldn't ever happen again. I told myself I was going to get stronger, get faster, and be the best, so I worked as hard as I could to get there. Also, I had more knowledge of the game. That's probably one of the most important things that came from the experience of getting on the field. It gave me a deeper understanding of the game, figuring out where my help was, knowing what my leverage was, knowing the best way to stay on top of a receiver so I don't get beat, but also knowing that I didn't have to worry about the rest of the field; I only had to deal with my receiver. Learning strategy and schemes became important, and pretty soon it was all second nature. I was still skinny, and I didn't really start to put on serious muscle weight until my junior year, but I was still a much better player, and people noticed.

There was another thing too. My sophomore year was the senior year of a kid named Damion Dixon, a wide receiver who was being recruited by a lot of top programs. He ended up going to the University of Louisville but transferred to McNeese State, both Division I schools, so he was big time. College coaches came from all over to scout him, and in practice, I was the one covering him every day. That was making me better too, covering the best receiver in practice, staying with him, learning how to defend a guy who was that fast and strong. A guy who was that good, even when he beats you, you learn from it. He made me better. Truth is, we made each other better, even if I was a couple years younger.

Interestingly, I think that's a good lesson for anyone. If you're trying to get better, if you're trying to excel, pit yourself against the best person you can find. It doesn't matter if they beat you over and over again if you can learn your craft better and improve your performance. Eventually, you're going to start getting some wins of your own, and that's only going to boost your confidence.

It was because of that improvement and knowledge that, right around then, the game started to slow down for me. Like I was faster than it was and I could see things coming. I understood schemes and patterns, different plays, different routes the receivers were going to run, all of that came much more naturally. Getting technical, if a guy lined up in the cut split—that is, close to the linemen rather than lined up wide toward the sidelines—I immediately knew he might run an out route, which would take him out wide (some of you have no idea what that means, but what's important is how easy I was able to recognize this stuff and react to it). Small things that never occurred to me before or that slipped past me didn't slip past me anymore. I caught them and was ready for them.

Just like that, I was the team's top corner, even though there were guys who were older than me. But my work ethic—always so, so important—and my dedication to the game made me better. The coaches recognized it, too.

Coach Blanchard again: "The thing I always knew about you is your work ethic and your character were both just so strong. The story I like, the one that I think defines you, happened in February of your freshman year. Damion Dixon was committing to Louisville, and there was a big celebration with the fans and the TV cameras and everything to watch Damion put on the hat of the school where he was going to go. Afterward, I saw you sitting there, I put my hand on your shoulder, and I said, 'You like this, kid?' I'll never forget what you said. You said, 'Don't worry about me, Coach. I'm gonna get my hat.' I knew from that moment you were going to succeed, and to this day, you are the most focused kid I ever coached. You always knew where you were going and what you were doing. We never thought we could put too much on you, that whatever we gave you you'd handle it just fine. You were so good defensively, we just knew early on that you were a special cat."

That doesn't mean I was always easy to coach, though. If someone wanted me to do something I didn't understand, I didn't just do it. I wanted to know why. Coach Blanchard understood this. He told me, "For me, you were incredibly easy to coach, but that wasn't universal. Coach Cummings had trouble with you because he wanted things done a certain way, and you would always ask why, and it irritated him. He would push, push, push you to try to get more out of you, but that's not your style. I would coach different kids differently. Some I'd get right in their grill, and others I'd leave alone, and you were the latter. If you remember, you even came to me and said, 'This is how I'd like to be coached.' I finally had to go to Cummings and say, 'Either coach him the way I'm asking you to do it, or just let me coach him. Whatever you need him to do, tell me.' You were such a thinker; there always had to be a rhyme and a reason to what we were doing. I enjoyed coaching you, but you were challenging to someone who wasn't tuned in to that."

That makes sense to me, and I think it's one of the reasons why I did so well in college, because I was surrounded by players and coaches who thought the same way, but I'll get to that soon enough.

I got my first scholarship offer from Tulane during the summer of my sophomore year when I went to a seven-on-seven football camp there, and I think that's probably when I got to be better known in the area. Around that same time, I started putting on more weight, too. I was up to about 160 as a sophomore, and after I turned sixteen, I started bulking up. And, of course, each summer I'd be back with Reggie Williams, working my butt off for the next season.

My athletic life revolved around football, it's true, but I also did well in track. I never *loved* it, but I kept doing it because I knew it would help with football, keep me running, and allow me to hold on to my edge. I was practical about it, just like I tried to be practical about everything. Track was a means to an end, you know? It was a tool, nothing more than that.

Another important lesson: sometimes you have to do things you don't love to make yourself better at the things you do love. Seems simple, but I've found it's pretty hard for people to understand, much less to do. For me, it was just part of everything else, working as hard as I could to get to where I needed to be. This was an important strategy in my life. It still is today.

I ran the 100 and 200 meters, sometimes the 400, but my junior and senior years we won the state title in the 4 X 200 relay. I wasn't even the fastest guy on the team, if you can believe it. There were two other guys who were faster and ended up getting track scholarships. My top time in the 100 was 10.6 seconds, which is fast but not world class. The other guys could do a 10.3 or 10.4. A couple tenths of a second might not seem like much, but in the world of sprinting, it's huge.

But football was the center of it all. The team was never great; we were always solid, but we never got over the hump. We made the playoffs my last two years but didn't get very far. Part of it was that we'd lose so many players. At least one guy I knew, a guy who was one of the best guys I ever played with, kept screwing up and ended up getting kicked out of school. He was just one, and there were plenty others just like him.

Junior year, I really started separating myself from everyone else. They got me the ball more often on offense, and receivers could not do anything against me on defense. I think I only allowed two or three completions all season. Scholarship offers started really coming in too. Nebraska, Tennessee, Ole Miss, big-time programs—they all offered scholarships, but I committed to Vanderbilt during my visit there with my mom. We both fell in love with the place, and she wanted me to go to the best school possible. That was Vandy, which is one of the best big schools in the country. I think I had about fifteen other offers overall, but Vandy was the best fit.

"When you went to visit Vanderbilt," Coach Blanchard told me, "the last thing I said to you before you left and I went on vacation was, 'Whatever you do, don't commit.' I pulled into the vacation house, the phone rang, my wife was about to kill me, but I said, 'It's Dre, I gotta take it.' And you said, 'I committed to Vanderbilt.' That you were so confident about your decision, that you were so immediately into it—that told me you were making the right choice. Once you were committed too, all the stress was off, and you had just a fantastic senior year."

No lie there. I *did* have a fantastic year. My senior year I shut everyone down. Literally. I did not give up a single pass completion all season. Not one. Sounds crazy, right? But it's true. Here, Coach Blanchard will back it up: "Yes, I will back up that claim. You did not give up a single pass completion your senior year. Not one."

I tell people that now, and they say I'm exaggerating, but obviously I'm not. I was that confident, knew I was that good and that nobody could beat me. I was also returning punts and kickoffs and playing receiver, but defensively, I was on a completely different level. You could not touch me, and I made sure you knew it.

When I was a freshman, a recruiter from Auburn was in our field house looking for Damion Dixon. And my coach introduced us by saying, "This is Andre Hal, and he's a freshman, but he is going to be a great player." The guy looked at me, this scrawny little kid, and kind of smiled. I remembered that, thinking, "I'm gonna show you." (In my junior year at Vandy, we actually beat Auburn, which never happens, and I reveled in that, but we'll get more into it in the college chapter). That's probably 85 percent of my life: "I'll show you. You don't believe I can do something? I'll show you. You don't think I can succeed? I'll show you." That was just one of the things I carried with me to get me to that place where I was so strong. I felt like I could shut down anyone, any time. I can't be the best? I can't stop you? I'll show you.

Coach Blanchard reminded me of a football camp at Alabama the summer before my senior year. A coach there kept telling him, "You gotta show Dre to Coach Saban. You gotta do it." Nick Saban has won more national championships than anyone and is maybe the best coach in college football. So we went to this camp, and I'll let Coach Blanchard tell the story from here.

"I took you to the Alabama camp before your senior year, and they told you that they already had a couple corners they'd had committed, but if either of them decommitted, you were going to get a scholarship offer. We went in to see Coach Saban, and Nick sat you down and said, 'You have what it takes. You have an ability to succeed and excel in where this game is going. You can play corner, or you can play safety,' and honestly, it was the first time I'd heard it or even considered it, you playing safety. And of course you ended up playing safety in the NFL. I think about that conversation all the time."

That was something, hearing from someone like Coach Saban that he thought I was that talented, but at the same time, I already knew it. I knew it because I had that chip on my shoulder that made me work harder than anyone else. I was ready for the next level. It was time to move on from Port Allen, to go somewhere else and transition into a new phase in my life.

I was ready to go. My situation wasn't terrible, but I knew it could be better. I knew I had a need to improve myself and grow up, and that wasn't going to happen if I stayed in Louisiana. My mom wanted me around, but she also saw what had happened to my dad by never really leaving his mom. I knew I needed to go off on my own and become the adult version of me. I needed to build my own life. I didn't want to be like my dad, never really leaving home or setting up his own life. I wanted and needed to leave.

My eighteenth birthday was May 30, 2010. My birthday party was also a going-away party. Right after that, in early June, I moved to Nashville for summer classes, to get acclimated to Vanderbilt, and to start training for the football season. The next chapter of my life was about to begin.

CHAPTER 5

Cancer

In the spring of 2018, I showed up for OTAs between my fourth and fifth seasons in the NFL. Things were fine. We'd had a lousy season as a team in 2017, but I'd had a great season personally. Aside from the huge contract I'd signed before the season started, which is worth a chapter all its own, I'd also just finished my best year, with five pass deflections, three interceptions, and a career high in tackles, with sixty-four.

The team was looking good for the upcoming season, though. We'd had two straight playoff seasons before the 4–12 year in 2017. This, by the way, was after getting to the second round of the playoffs the year before, ultimately losing to the New England Patriots, who had gone on to win the Super Bowl. And in that game against the Pats, it's important to note that Tom Brady, probably the greatest quarterback in the history of the game, the guy who has won six Super Bowls, threw two interceptions.

I made one of them. That's right, I picked off the GOAT in a playoff game (which is the kind of thing I can someday share with my grandchildren), then I followed it up with maybe the best year I had in the NFL, so coming into OTAs for the 2018 season, my hopes were high, as were my expectations.

But then, one morning, I woke up and my vision was blurry. I also had a headache. I figured maybe I'd had my bell rung in practice the day before, so I didn't say anything to anyone; I just went back into practice. I was a football player. I just figured I'd play through it because that's what football players do. You gut it out. You go out with the team and try not to think too much about it.

If you're sensing a pattern with my behavior here—not talking, not asking for help, being afraid to show "weakness," refusing to learn from earlier mistakes—that's because it's exactly what I was doing. It's what we all do, isn't it? Repeat unhealthy behavior? It's human nature. I mean, how many times does something have to happen, how many times do we have to do something wrong before we finally listen? Before we learn? Before we actually change our behavior? And what is it that finally *makes* us listen?

In my case, it was blurry vision and a headache that kept me from actually seeing the football and doing my job. And try as I might, there was no way I could keep ignoring it because it wasn't going away on its own. Even worse, my balance was off, and when I did see the ball, I either couldn't catch it or I couldn't hold on to it. This went on for a couple days, and when it was even getting a bit worse on day three,

I finally went to see the trainers. I told them, "Man, I can't see a damn thing. My eyes are trippin.'" On top of that, my left eye was drooping, which...well, it wasn't anywhere close to normal.

They sent me to the eye doctor, and at first, he thought I had cataracts. I've heard that doctors sometimes prescribe marijuana for help with cataracts, but I wasn't so lucky. Instead of pot, I got contact lenses. My vision had always been perfect, so the need for the contacts was jarring. They were also difficult for me to handle. It took me close to an hour to get them in place.

This only lasted two days because I knew it wasn't helping. My eyes were still blurred, I still couldn't really see. Something wasn't right. I went back to the trainers, who sent me back to the eye doctor, who took another look at me and sent me right to the hospital.

Now I was starting to wonder what was really going on. The *hospital*? Come on. What could be wrong with me? What was the big deal?

At first, they didn't know. They tested me, gave me an MRI, checked my brain, ran me through some other tests, and then sent me home. So there I was, sitting at home, chillin,' waiting to receive some news about what was happening, when I got the call from the trainers, who said I needed to get to the stadium immediately. I asked why, of course. I tried to get them to tell me what the deal was, but they just insisted I come over and we'd talk when I got there.

So I got in my car and drove over. I remember I had to keep one eye closed so I could see straight because by then the blurriness had worsened. It'd moved from blurriness to double vision. I had both hands on the wheel, one eye closed, and my head slightly tilted to one side so I could see where the heck I was going.

Once I got there, I walked into the trainers' room and saw my head coach, Bill O'Brien, waiting for me with the trainers. I looked around and saw that everyone was really upset, and Coach was downright distraught. That's when I stopped and said, "Okay, what the hell is really going on?" I still thought I was fine. I was just having a little problem with my eyes, but it was clearly much worse than that. I knew it just from seeing Coach's face. I'd never seen him like that, and nobody was answering me. Finally, the head trainer, who was saying, "Oh my God..." told me that the tests found lesions on my brain.

I had no idea what this meant. I asked to see the scans, and they showed me one. There it was, right on the scan, plain as day: something on the left side of my brain. Apparently, it was pushing against my optical nerve, causing my eye to droop, my vision to blur, and the headaches that were bothering me.

That's when they told me I needed to get back to the hospital ASAP. So they took me to the hospital to do more tests. I did another MRI, they took blood, and then more blood, and then some more blood, then they did another brain scan. They kept analyzing the blood, but the tests kept coming back normal. But then the brain scan came back, and they said that they saw something on my brain, something more than the first lesion they saw—but they weren't sure what it was. They just knew it didn't look good.

I stayed in the hospital for three or four days, just taking test after test. They tapped my spine, and they found a rise in my white blood cell count, which they thought indicated some kind of infection. It wasn't super high, but it was higher than normal, and high enough to make them a little worried. At first, they didn't think it was anything too bad. They just started asking how I was feeling, and I said I was actually feeling better. They gave me some steroids, and those actually helped. My balance went back to normal, and my vision improved. They kept me there another couple of days, and I started getting fed up with it. I was eager to leave.

That's when they told me I needed to go to MD Anderson Cancer Center. "MD Anderson? *Cancer*? I'm sorry, but…what?"

They thought maybe I had cancer. First, they thought I had sarcoidosis, which is an inflammatory disease that mostly affects the lungs and the lymph nodes, but they dismissed that pretty quickly and thought instead that it might be cancer.

I have something on my brain, and it might be cancer. That's when I said, "Oh, shit."

I wondered, and asked aloud, whether it could possibly be some kind of concussion-related thing. From football? I'd certainly been hit a few times. I'd never actually been diagnosed with a concussion, but it was possible, right? It had to be some kind of football-related injury.

No, they told me. It's not from football.

Well, it's my brain, *what else could it be from?* They kept beating around the bush, trying to figure out what it could be, doing more tests, checking me out over and over again. They put me in an ambulance, took me over to MD Anderson, and then it was another three days of tests, tests, and more tests. I asked, "Am I sick or what? Tell me what is going on so we can fix this and I can go home." People were asking me where I was, what was going on. My teammates were checking on me because I wasn't at work. People wanted to know what was happening, and I didn't know what to tell them.

I voiced this frustration to the doctors and said I was going to split. They were shocked at this. They asked me what I was talking about. I was just going to get up and *leave*? Well, that got them running around, and they called the Texans, told them what I was planning, and the head trainer called me and asked me to stay for one more day of tests. I didn't want to stay one minute longer. I felt great. I didn't realize how much the steroids were helping, obviously, but I was convinced I was fine.

Whatever it was, it was exhausting. The swelling on my brain was some kind of inflammation, but if they didn't know what it was, what good were they? It was infuriating. That's when I realized that doctors don't have all the answers. They're really just practicing on people. Literally, their work is called "a practice," and I was sick and tired of being "practiced" on, getting stuck with needles, constantly being poked and prodded, so I said I was getting the hell out of there and I would figure out for myself what was wrong with me.

The day before I was planning to leave, they finally came back and said they wanted to do a biopsy of a swollen lymph node they'd found under my armpit. I couldn't feel it, but they insisted that it was there, and they needed to go in and have it checked out.

The results came back that I had Hodgkin lymphoma. I remember saying, "That's cancer, but how can that be? I'm fine. I feel fine. I feel great, even. Cancer is this incredibly serious thing, but I don't feel like there's anything wrong with me, especially since my headaches and eye issues cleared up."

My mom was with me, and we both were shocked by it. We just couldn't believe it. How was this possible?

I know this is a common response for people when they're diagnosed with this disease, but usually there's actually something wrong with them. I know I'd had those issues that got me to the hospital in the first place, but those had gone away, and the lesions on my brain seemed to be healing, so it wasn't just denial. Still, I understand the denial, especially from someone in my shoes. I was twenty-five years old, just about to turn twenty-six, in the peak of physical condition, a world-class athlete, and I'm being told that my body has betrayed me? Of course I'm not going to believe it. Of course I'm going to look around and try to find another answer.

But my not believing it was there didn't make it disappear. Clearly it was there, so we asked them what the next step was. They suggested chemotherapy. Right away. I said I didn't want chemo in my brain, and they said, no, it doesn't work that way. What would happen is that they would put the chemo into my spine, that it would take care of whatever was on my brain. This freaked me out. I didn't want to put the port into my body. I didn't want to use their medicines. They wanted to make sure my brain was okay, but I play football: a lot of players have some sort of problem with their brains.

I know that sounds...cavalier. I certainly don't take it lightly, but there are certain risks you take playing football that you're well aware of when you're in the middle of it. Possible brain injuries almost come with the territory. So in this case,

I thought, "Okay, let's figure out the best way to handle this, but I don't want chemo to be a part of the solution."

At the very least, now they knew what the issue was. One problem solved. Now to solve the other one: making me healthy again. The doctors told me that I probably wouldn't play football that season, that I would be out for a year, but I wasn't having that at all.

That's another thing I think lots of cancer patients come to: the decision to fight and beat the thing back, to triumph over the disease and prove the doctors wrong. This idea, this concept of defiance, it goes right along with denial. To respond negatively to bad news is an incredibly human thing, isn't it? To be told that something horrible has happened, of course the instinct is to say, "No. Not me. It's not true." But then when they tell you, "Yes, it is true. It is real," it's just as instinctual to say, "Well, I'm going to beat it. I don't care how long you say I'm going to be out or how hard it's going to be, *I am better than this, stronger than this, and I will triumph.* No two ways about it."

I think it's even more common when it happens to someone like me, someone whose whole life, whose whole career, happens because of physical abilities. It's not like I worked in an office eight hours a day. I made my money because of what I could do on a football field, and now here came cancer to try to screw that up for me.

But I convinced myself that I wasn't going to let it. I refused to give the disease that much power over me. Was that hubris? Some irrational overconfidence? My whole life was based on having the confidence to know that I was unbeatable. That I was the best. How could I think any differently, even against a formidable opponent like this?

I decided I wanted to tell the team myself. I left the hospital and went to practice, got up in front of the guys, and told them what was going on. I never used the word *cancer*, but I did say I had Hodgkin lymphoma and that even though the doctors said I probably would be out for the year, I swore I'd be back within six months, which would allow me to play the second half of the season. I made a promise to them and to myself that I was going to be back this year. I even said it just like that. "I will be back this year. I am not going to let this beat me. I'm going to beat it."

My teammates were great. They did exactly what I knew they would: they backed me, supported me, and told me they were there however and whenever I might need them. It was incredibly gratifying. I am still grateful to them today.

The next day I went back to the hospital and asked when I could start working out again. They said I needed to take a couple weeks to heal from the biopsy, but more immediately, we needed to talk about treatment options if I wasn't going to do chemo. I reminded them once again that there was just no way I was going to let them put a chemo port inside me to deliver that poison into my body.

I asked if there was something else they could try, and they suggested an experimental drug called Rituxan. That sounded good to me, so I said sure, let's go for it. I needed to come in for a treatment once a week for four weeks, starting immediately. They warned me it wasn't going to be easy, that once the Rituxan hit the tumor, once it hit the lymph node, I would start shaking and my body would react pretty intensely to it. But I said I understood and that I was ready for whatever came.

The treatment takes six hours. They hook you up to an IV, and you just sit there. The first time I took it I watched some Netflix and did some reading and waited for the negative side effects to start happening, but they just never did. I simply had no reaction at all. Nothing. I was fine. I'd go home, do some yoga, hang out, and after a couple weeks, when I was allowed to start working out again, I did that too. Pretty soon I was working out with the team in the morning, then would drive myself over to MD Anderson and, afterward, drive myself home. My body was completely fine through the whole process. I kept the same routine the whole time, which helped because the yoga and meditation kept my mind focused on what I had to do to get through the situation I was in and beat the disease.

So for four weeks, I did this. Drove to the hospital, got treatment, went home, mixed in workouts when I could, saw the team when I could, and then, at week five, I went back in, and the doctor says, "The cancer is gone, but we still see this stuff in your brain." They did another MRI, and it showed that I still had the lesions but that they were healing, so the doctors wanted me to keep on the Rituxan because they thought that's what was taking care of the lesions.

But the thing was that since I wasn't taking part in full team activities, I had some time, and I had started looking into more natural methods of treatment. I found that improving the body's immune system doesn't just go a long way to fighting off disease, it also helps the body heal. Knowing my body as well as I did and seeing how it had dealt with the cancer in my system, I wanted to test the idea that it could continue to fix itself in the most natural way possible without putting any of the more conventional (and often very toxic) medicines into my body.

This was another important lesson. The body's immune system is an incredible machine. There are obviously times when it's overwhelmed no matter how well you take care of it, but if you can nurture it and take care of it, it will take care of you. That is what I had been doing my whole life, and it's something anyone can do, really. Think about how you treat your body. Exercise. Eat healthy food. Be aware. These are small things on their own, but you add them up, and they have a huge and direct impact on your overall health and well-being, not just physically but on emotional and spiritual levels too. Again, I was a professional athlete playing maybe the most difficult physical sport there is, and I was one of the best in the world at it. But no matter where you are in life or what you do, *you can always be a better version of yourself.* If you're a little overweight, lose a couple pounds. Don't get enough exercise? Start trying to walk a little bit each day or bike ride. Not the healthiest eater? Make the decision to cut down on the junk food. None of this is that hard, and all of it will help your body in the long run.

One of the things I'd found that so heavily contributes to the strength of your immune system is vitamin C. So when they told me they wanted to keep me on the Rituxan, I told them I was going to pass on that and instead do my own thing. This is not something I recommend for everyone, but it was the right choice for me. I started getting IV infusions of vitamin C. I bought a hyperbaric chamber. I started eating better. I hired a chef and specialized my diet. The doctors had cleared me of cancer, but the team wouldn't let me play right away because of the lesions that were still on my brain, even though they'd been shrinking. I missed the rest of OTAs, obviously, but then I missed all of training camp, and the season was starting, and I still wasn't on the field.

So I keep doing my all-natural thing, spending time in the hyperbaric chamber, eating right, doing yoga, meditating, and I'm waiting for the go-ahead so I can start playing again. I ask, they say no. I ask again, they say no again. I ask one more time, they keep saying no. I still have the lesions on my brain, they tell me. They're smaller, but they're still there.

Months go by. They had said that the minimum amount of time it was going to take me to get back was six months. They didn't even think I'd play the whole year, but now I was dead set on coming back before then. The thing was, they kept saying I wasn't ready. So, one day, after a few months, I went in and said I needed another MRI, that I was having headaches and wanted to see if there was anything wrong, like last time.

I just wanted to see what my brain looked like. I went to an imaging center in Lafayette, Louisiana, had a brain scan, and they came back and asked me why I was there because my brain was normal. There was nothing wrong with it. The lesions were gone. I was clean. I was relieved, thrilled that I could finally relax. There had been so much pressure on me, and I so badly wanted to get back on the field, so when I learned that I was okay, I was relieved and thankful and ready to get back into action.

Well, now it was time for me to get back on the field. The season had started, I'd missed games, and I didn't want to miss any more of them. I went to the Texans and demanded they reinstate me, and if they didn't, I was walking away and I wouldn't come back. (Little did we all know that this was foreshadowing of something that would actually happen.) They finally started listening to me, said they'd see what was going on, that they had to get me checked out, but I told them I'd already had my brain scanned and showed them that I was all clear. So there was no reason to hold me back anymore.

It took two days of me sitting at home and waiting, but they finally called me up and said I was cleared to play. Oh. Okay. *Now* I'm clear, after I did all this work on my own to prove it instead of the team taking care of me. I actually went off. I lost my temper, which is not like me at all. I don't get angry like that, and I especially don't yell at people, but I went into the trainers' room and let loose.

I was just so frustrated, so tired of not being able to play, so annoyed that I had to take it in my own hands. But when I said that, when I gave them the ultimatum, they just said okay, and all of a sudden, I was back on the field. Remember, this was also the week that my dad died, so that certainly had something to do with my state of mind, but the fact was, the team dropped the ball, and I had to pick it up.

I'm a firm believer in being able to talk to others, to ask for help when needed, admitting you're wrong, taking responsibility...I've talked about all of this, I will continue to talk about it, and I mean every word. But at the same time, it's also true that you have to be your own biggest defender and strongest advocate. Ask questions. Investigate. Explore your options, figure out your next steps, then *take* those steps. Of course, there are some kinds of cancer that aren't going to be healed in the same way that mine was—every case and every person is different—but there are plenty of other things that can either be prevented or healed by less conventional methods. If you are in a bad situation, there is almost always a way out of it. It's up to you to find that way. No one else is going to do it for you. Both the choice and the resulting action belong to you and you alone.

In my case, the doctors told me that I should do chemotherapy, and if I hadn't asked why, if I hadn't investigated other avenues, I would have gone ahead with it, and it probably wouldn't have turned out the way it did. They wanted to keep me on an experimental drug that, admittedly, had helped me, but it turned out that I didn't need that either and my body bounced back faster without it.

The lesson is not that conventional health care methods don't work. That would be inaccurate. Of course they work, under the right circumstances. The lesson is that there are usually other options, and you should always explore them, then choose the best one for you. Doctors know a lot, but they don't know everything. If you're sick, then it is literally your life that's on the line, so you should be doing as much work as possible to find the best treatment for you.

Just like the other lessons I've talked about in this book, this one crosses over into the rest of life. Exploring options, learning as much as you can about a given situation, finding the best option for you, all of this applies in everyday life. It works for your career, it works for your personal life, it works in just about every aspect of existence. It sort of ties into the idea of having a good work ethic, if you think about it, because it also involves getting down and dirty into the details, even if it's not always pleasant. It might not be pleasant, but you'll be better off every time. Guaranteed.

So now I was back on the field, I had just buried my dad, and I had been working out so much and been under so much stress, I was actually worn down in spite of the fact that I was probably in the best shape of my whole life. After that first game, the media kept asking me how I was, and the answer was always the same: *I was fine.* I'd been fine for a while and had been ready to get back on the field. In fact, getting back on the field earlier would have been great for me. It would have been a really good psychological and emotional treatment, letting me get back on the field to do what I was getting paid to do. But for whatever reason, the team was reluctant.

Of course, in my first game back, against Jacksonville in Week Six, I fractured my shoulder, which cost me two games right after that. But then I came back and played in the last seven games of the season. Shoulder aside, I was fine. I was healthy. I had lost my starting job, but that was natural, and I did play plenty. I also ended up starting two games before the end of the season. As I mentioned before, in just half a season, I still tied for the team lead with three interceptions. Not bad for a guy who'd had cancer and lesions on his brain just a few months before.

The thing was, though, I continued to be bothered by the amount of drama I had to go through to get back on the field. It wasn't sitting right with me. I felt that I wasn't getting the whole truth. If I was okay to play but didn't get the green light until I badgered them about it, then was almost immediately cleared…well, I can't be the only one who thinks that's strange.

I was a long way from considering the retirement that was, obviously, right around the corner, but I did start to question the circumstances I was in. I couldn't be in a system where they can tell me who I am and what I've got, what I can and can't do. Especially when it's no longer a system I fully trust. I said I was ready to play, they said I wasn't. I threatened them with an ultimatum, and they finally caved and said, "Okay, maybe you're ready to play after all." Something else was going on there.

The word *disease* comes from the fact that your body is literally in a state of dis-ease. But my body wasn't at dis-ease. It was in top form. I was in spectacular shape. Maybe if I'd felt lousy, I'd have thought differently about it, but the fact that my body was so strong made all the difference. Honestly, since I left the doctor's office after my last scan, I haven't been back.

I will talk more about how dealing with cancer changed me and my own sense of spirituality in a bit because it ended up being directly involved with my decision to retire, but first I think it's important to close this chapter on my particular experience with the disease and the lessons I learned from it.

I think that part of my success in fighting the disease so successfully was my absolute refusal to accept that it was going to kill me. Honestly, I never really accepted the fact that I had it at all. When they told me, my mom and I both just rejected it. Did that have anything to do with how quickly it disappeared? I like to think it did. And knowing how powerful the mind can be, I do think one is related to the other.

For me, it was about getting my body back to a state of ease, and my frame of mind was integral to that process. If I had gone down the path of self-doubt and self-pity, I never would have recovered as quickly as I did. I'm 100 percent certain of that. Instead, I knew for sure that I was going to beat it, that I was going to come back and play again, and that I was going to do it in less time than the doctors told me it was going to take. And I did.

I told myself I was in control of it, and that changed everything. I know that not everyone can do this and that there are some cancers, some diseases, that are far more serious and deadly than the one I battled and beat, but the power of the mind is incredible, and the right attitude can go a long way. Being positive in the face of a crisis can make all the difference, whether it's personal or professional. Trouble at work? Major crisis occurring and you're not sure what's going to happen? A positive attitude and belief in yourself will help you get through it. A sickness or health issue? Same thing. If you tell yourself you're going to be okay by going deep into your soul and *affirming* that you will beat whatever challenge is standing in your way, this is what will get you—and keep you—in the right mindset. And when it comes to your health, headspace is everything. I know it is for me.

The point is to try to stay in control. That's what I kept telling myself. "I am in control of this." And that's how I took it. Look, I realize I had certain advantages. I had the money to pay for those vitamin C treatments, which weren't cheap. The hyperbaric chamber cost $10,000, and I was willing to spend that money to get me healthy and back on the field. But there are plenty of less expensive answers for those who don't have the kinds of resources I had.

My point is that when given bad news or a bad diagnosis, don't just listen to "the experts." Investigate the problem yourself. Find the best answers for you. Make sure you're knowledgeable about your situation and are as well informed about it as anyone, including the people offering to treat you. Their priorities may overlap with yours, but they're not the same because for them, there are other factors. For you, the only factor, literally the only one, is your survival. That's why, sure, it's okay to depend on others, but when it comes right down to it, *you* need to be your own best advocate.

Like I mentioned earlier, when I was diagnosed, my mom and I looked at each other and just didn't believe it. The doctors were surprised that neither of us were crying or seemed sad, but we both had the same reaction, which was, "What can we do? What's next? What's the process to beat it?" That was our instinctive reaction. Everything I've been talking about, all the attitude and belief and confidence, they all go hand in hand. So does work ethic. Good work ethic, working your butt off, it has everything to do with all the other things I've been talking about here. In a sense, it's all one and the same.

The last thing I'll say here is that beating cancer gave me a new kind of confidence. It added a newer, stronger layer to what I already had. Now I knew I could do anything I set my mind to doing—on the field *and* off—which eventually paved the way for me to walk away from the only life I'd ever really known.

CHAPTER 6

Vanderbilt

As I said before, I graduated from high school, turned eighteen, and then headed off to college, all back-to-back. I wanted to get acclimated and get ready for football, and getting out of Port Allen was really good for me, so off I went to Nashville, Tennessee.

The thing about summer school is it's a fluke. It made me think I was capable of actually succeeding at Vanderbilt because I immediately thought it would be that easy throughout the whole semester. It gave me a false sense of security, really. Fewer students and a bunch of football players, so I thought it'd be all good. I had my first two classes, I got into the rhythm of working out as a college athlete, doing that in the morning and class in the afternoon. It wasn't as strict as I thought it would be, but like I said, it was the summertime, so it was very laid back. I met four of my best friends that summer: Jordan Matthews, Karl Butler, Kenny Landler, and Jonathan Krause. We were all there together that first summer. It was a great time, and I thought I was prepared for when classes started in the fall.

Boy, was I wrong. That fall shocked the hell out of me. I didn't know *what* was going on because all of a sudden school got so tough and I didn't know what I was doing. I had no idea how to maneuver, and after pretty much coasting through high school, I didn't really know how to study. There was also something else, a subtle thing that I didn't necessarily realize at the time but something that definitely had an effect on me: I didn't know how to talk to people or how to network. The idea of approaching other students was hard for me, at least partially because I felt intimidated. It just wasn't a pattern that I was accustomed to.

For the first time in my life, I was being challenged, and I started having doubts about whether I was smart enough to stay there at Vandy. Sure, I may have been a great football player with serious prospects to play in the NFL, but I was also a scared college freshman wondering if I had what it took to stick around at one of the best schools in the country. Looking around and seeing these other kids who seemed to have it all figured out, I was afraid to approach them for help or to study together because I was afraid they'd think I was dumb. That I was just some football player who didn't belong in the same classes with them.

The thing about guys who go to college to play football is that many of them (not all, but many) go to college to play football, not to be students. That's the truth for a big chunk of the guys who come through, but I didn't want it to be true for me. Going to a school like Vanderbilt meant something to me, and I wanted to succeed, but almost immediately after that first fall semester started, I realized I was in way over my head, and I didn't know how to ask for help. And the thing about Vandy, unlike some other big schools, is that they actually *care* if you go to class. They don't care how good an athlete you are—the academics are far more important.

If a paper was due on a certain day, you weren't getting an extension just because you were on the football team. Maybe some of the professors were even harder on you because of it. At Vanderbilt, you were a student first and an athlete second, even though the coaches thought it was the other way around. This only meant we had to go hard on the field *and* in the classroom. Part of the problem too was that I was barely playing as a freshman, which pissed me off, and I wasn't really mature enough yet to handle that, so it only added to the problems.

It was all a bit too much for me at first, and since I couldn't bring myself to talk to my classmates and I had a hard time talking to anyone else and saying how much trouble I was having, I started thinking about just packing it in and walking away, heading back to Port Allen, and doing something else. I went to Vanderbilt thinking it was going to be okay, but it was so much harder than I thought, and the doubts were so strong, I felt lost. Alone. Isolated. Frustrated. It was only October of my freshman year, and I was thinking of going home.

Of course, once I mentioned this to my mom, she woke me up pretty quickly, telling me I wasn't coming home, that I'd never been a quitter, that she hadn't raised a quitter, that I had worked too long and too hard to just walk away, and that

I was going to have to figure things out and come home with a degree from Vanderbilt just like we'd agreed. That was a big part of getting me turned around, but there were two other things too. The first was not wanting to prove the doubters right. There were people back in Louisiana who didn't think I was going to make it, who thought I wasn't good enough, wasn't smart enough, or just didn't have it.

This, by the way, is part of human nature. (Some humans, anyway.) There will always be the naysayers, the doubters, the people who want others to fail, because if others fail, it somehow makes them feel better about themselves and their own failures. It's important not to let those people into your life, but sometimes you can't help it. Maybe they're part of your family or they have some other deeper connection to you, but the trick is to not allow them to make you lack belief in yourself. Don't let them have that much power over you. Understand that their desire to see you fail has nothing really to do with you and everything to do with them, even if it doesn't feel like it when they're telling you how incapable you are of succeeding.

You may think it's easy for me to say that, but I feel entitled to say it because, for the first time in my life, I was struggling, and so I was open to those doubts and susceptible to the feelings of vulnerability and, yep, even fear that went with them. Suddenly, for the first time, there was space in my head for the idea that I might not make it, ideas placed in my head by the people who actively wanted me to fail. Once my mom snapped me awake and reminded me of how hard I'd worked to get to this place, I reminded myself that these people had been telling me this stuff my whole life. I was too small. I wasn't fast enough. I couldn't make it on the big stage. I never believed them before, but suddenly I was believing them now? No, once I wrapped my head around all that, I felt better. I wasn't going to let them make me doubt myself anymore. I was going to push through and make it.

Some might call that a fear of failure. I call it an exercise in empowerment. Whatever it was, it worked. I'd faced enough adversity already in my life, had been told—and had told myself—that the cream rises to the top, and so I knew I'd have to step it up and do it for myself, just like I always had. If I put my mind to it, I'd be able to figure it out. Even though I was failing one of my classes, if I worked my butt off, I would find a way to make it.

This would help me in the long run too because it hammered home the idea that if I put my mind to something, really gave it my full focus, I could accomplish it. I saw other students getting it done, I saw my teammates getting it done, so why couldn't I? People played football and still graduated every single year, and if they could do it, I could too. There wasn't anything that someone else could do that I couldn't. So that's what I did. I put my head down, and I started grinding it out. I did what had to be done to meet my goal.

The second thing that changed it for me was meeting two women who would change my life. The first was a woman named Laurie Woods. She is a sociology professor and student advisor, and I'd taken one of her classes that first summer session. She and I had clicked, and I really responded to her as a teacher. Apparently it was reciprocal because she saw me struggling and she reached out to me to give me some guidance and to remind me that I belonged there. She was the one who got me on the right path. I was quiet, didn't talk much, but she'd seen something in me. Seen who I was and that I needed help. She came to me first and talked me through everything. She showed me that I could be successful at Vanderbilt. If she weren't there, I don't know where I'd be right now, to be honest. She actually helped guide me through that journey.

I still talk to Laurie all the time, so I asked her about how she remembers this, and she said, "I don't specifically recall a moment where I approached you, but here's the thing: Vanderbilt is a hard school to get into, but it's a harder school to stay in. And the athletes who get in are smart, but then they're surrounded suddenly by academic superstars, and they're made to feel dumb, and a lot of their professors just add on to that. So they struggle with that identity, of having to go to class, and the football player part is less important.

"The thing I remember about you," she continued, "is that you were smart enough to be there, you just didn't believe it. Now you totally believe it, but back then you didn't. What I saw in you was a solidness. You were a very solid person, very nice, with a quiet determination that I found very appealing. I told you that you belong here, that all you had to do was work hard and you could stay. Vanderbilt is into keeping people, and it was just about making you feel like you were more than just a member of a mediocre football team."

Once Laurie helped me get myself straightened out, I started opening up and talking to people. It was the first time I'd ever had to step out of my way to ask for help and guidance. My whole life I'd always guided myself. I was a self-starter, didn't have to be asked to do things, just always got it done on my own. But now, for the first time, I needed people to help me transition through this tough time. I needed someone to come in and tell me, "This is how you do it," and Laurie was that person for me. It changed my life, no question, and got me to open my mouth to ask questions and then be able to shut up and listen.

After my freshman year, the football coaching staff was fired, and the school hired James Franklin to come in as the head coach. He's at Penn State now, but in the winter of 2011, he took over a lousy Vanderbilt team and basically changed the whole culture there. We had two wins and ten losses my freshman year and came in last in the Eastern Division of the Southeastern Conference (SEC). Coach Franklin's first year, my second, we won six and lost seven. My last two years, we won nine and lost four. That's a pretty huge swing, and it says a lot about him and his abilities as a coach. All three years he was there (he left after the 2013 season, same as I did), we went to a Bowl game, and he's had great success at Penn State since he started there in 2014.

He didn't start until about mid-February of 2011, but once he did, we went right into training mode. It wasn't the same as during the season because the NCAA rules didn't allow us to practice the same way, but he instilled a new way of doing things at Vandy—and a new attitude—which made the whole team think differently. It was actually perfect timing for me, personally, because I was starting to feel a little more comfortable in my classes and my grades were improving. I was on academic probation after my first semester because I'd failed a class, but now that I had a better understanding of college life and had learned to communicate more effectively with others, I was locked in. Then things got much better, quickly.

The second woman I met who changed my life was someone who started out as a friend, became my girlfriend, and was a major positive influence in my life. Isis Freeman and I met first semester and stayed together all through college, up through my first year in the NFL. Isis is maybe the smartest person I've ever known. Ended up going to Harvard Law School and now works as a lawyer in Los Angeles. She's brilliant. Pretty much a genius. And she helped me immensely with my schoolwork and maneuvering through college. She read my papers and gave me notes, helped me learn the right way to study, taught me how to think about things and analyze them more clearly, taught me how to be a student, basically. She was my help and my aid at all times.

I'd write a paper; she'd read it and not let me turn it in until it was good enough to turn in. She'd help me revise it so that it would sound more "Vanderbilt." I didn't sound too Vanderbilt when I first got there, which shouldn't come as a surprise. I sounded like Port Allen. But Isis had her act together, and she helped me get my act together too. She was the perfect version of a personal tutor. That was Isis.

So basically, thanks to Laurie and Isis, two incredible women, I stayed in college and ended up doing pretty well while I was there. It was also the first time I learned that it was okay to ask for help, knowing that I couldn't get it all done totally on my own. It was the first time I learned that no one can, really. It's not possible. Again, this wasn't an admission of my own weakness but an acceptance of my own strength.

But the reality was this: I was also at Vanderbilt to play football, and there was a new coach and a new system in place. I spent the summer in Nashville taking classes—I basically never went home and stuck around campus as much as possible—and as my sophomore year began, I knew I had the chance to step it up, get more playing time, and make a positive impact. I was finally comfortable as a college student, so that part of my life had settled in. Now it was time to do it on the football field.

I got a lot more playing time in my sophomore year, but I think I was still only on the field for about a third of the snaps. There was one senior and one junior ahead of me on the depth chart. The senior was Casey Hayward, who ended up being drafted in the second round of the 2012 NFL Draft by Green Bay, and the junior was Trey Wilson, who also eventually played in the NFL. Trey and I competed for the second corner spot behind Casey, but I actually think the only reason he got more playing time than me is because he's older. It frustrated me because I genuinely thought I was better than Trey. I understood not playing as much as a freshman, but I'd made big steps forward as a sophomore and believed I had earned more playing time. So instead of complaining about it, I decided to keep my mouth shut and just work harder.

Yes, the pattern continues, and I am going to keep repeating it because it is worth repeating: work ethic is everything. It's the secret to just about any aspect of success, the key to unlock any problem, and it has certainly helped me unlock just about all of mine. Working my butt off got me to Vanderbilt. It got me to the NFL. And, as you just read last chapter, it helped me beat cancer. It was the same thing here. I just kept grinding and grinding, and I always tried staying humble. In this case, it wasn't too hard because I wasn't starting, but telling myself to keep my head down and work my butt off seemed like the right answer to the problem. It still is today.

It helped that I understood what Coach Franklin was bringing to the program. Maybe because a big part of it was a sense of discipline and a continual striving for excellence. Vanderbilt is not known for its football program. Yes, it's in the SEC, which is arguably the strongest in college football—with perennial powers like Alabama, Auburn, Florida, Georgia, and LSU—and it sends guys to the NFL every year, but it usually has a losing season and rarely has a winning record in conference games. That changed in Coach Franklin's first year, when we finished with six wins and six losses before losing in the Liberty Bowl, which was only the second Bowl game Vandy had been invited to in almost thirty years. As I mentioned before, he was there two more years, and we went to Bowls both times. That's three times in three years before he went to Penn State. Pretty good.

As you can imagine, that was my kind of thing, and I loved it. I loved everything about this new attitude, and if I'd been playing more, it would have been perfect. Still, I saw a really bright future for myself there and knew things would improve in my junior and senior years.

My defensive backfield coach was Bob Shoop, who now has the same job at the University of Michigan. He came in with Coach Franklin, and I got along with him right from the start. I asked him about our experience together those three years.

"I think you were on the field more than a third of the time sophomore year, but okay," he told me. "You always had the tools, that was obvious. Your sophomore year was our first year at Vanderbilt. James Franklin brought in a new attitude, and you bought right into that. You were an integral part of that culture. I think it took one meeting with you to realize you had your act together. That first meeting wasn't about football, it was about life, and you made a very good first impression. You were very driven and confident. I'm not going to say you had it all figured out, you were a freshman in college, but I was pretty sure you were something special. You were all in. It didn't take a lot to get you there."

Oh, and don't take my word for it about the work ethic part. Here's what he had to say about my sophomore year: "The guys ahead of you were playing at a super high level, but you still worked your way into the mix, and that says a lot about your work ethic and talent."

See? It's not just me talking about it, it's other people noticing it too. That kind of thing matters. I'll repeat this for you too: This isn't just about football. Developing a strong work ethic and an unshakable sense of self confidence will benefit you in absolutely every other walk of life. Work your butt off, do good work, believe in yourself, and people will notice. Don't believe me? Try it, then we'll talk.

Anyway, by the time junior year came along, Casey had graduated and was playing in Green Bay, and I had jumped ahead of Trey to become the team's top corner, covering the other team's best receivers. Now that I was given the chance to play and excel, I grabbed the opportunity and ran with it. The coaches weren't the only ones who saw it in my play;

the rest of the league did too. I was one of the best defensive backs in the entire SEC, and by the end of the season, I was named second team All-Conference. That meant that I was considered to be one of the top three or four cornerbacks in the league.

"I don't know if you remember this exact moment," Coach Shoop told me, "but your breakout game was against Tennessee at home in 2012, your junior year. We were watching film, a play came up, and I told you, 'They're gonna run this play tomorrow, you're gonna intercept it, and the SEC is going to make you Defensive Player of the Week.' And that's exactly what happened. I think you had two picks that day."

The confidence I'd always had on the football field, the confidence my dad had helped to instill inside me, was now translating off the field too. I wanted to be one of the best corners in the conference, and I was. I wanted to excel in school, get better grades, and feel like I had a home at Vanderbilt, and I did. I wasn't making all A's or anything, but I was doing well in school, and my academic probation days were way behind me.

The other thing this extra confidence helped me with was talking to my classmates. Fitting in. Being a part of college. I was really shy at first. I know that sounds strange, but I was. It took me a long time to work up the nerve to talk to other students because I didn't think they wanted to talk to me. Once I got myself across that bridge, though, I found they were really cool. They liked that I was a football player and were happy to help when I needed notes or to fill in the blanks when I had to miss class.

As Laurie Woods said, football players are often made to feel dumb, even when it's clear that we're not. This is exactly right and just how I felt until I came out of my shell. No two ways about it: there is a stigma attached to being a college football player, especially at a school with as good a reputation as Vandy. It's sort of a double-edged sword because football players take advantage of the benefits, for sure, but we also feel that stigma and can be insecure about the academic part of it. I certainly was, and when I look back, it makes a lot of sense to me, especially when someone like Laurie weighs in and backs it up.

If I have any real regret about my time at Vanderbilt, it's that I didn't make enough of an effort to find friends outside of football. Part of my problem in that area is that I was so locked in on the game. I wanted to make it to the NFL, and the better I did on the field at Vandy, the better chance I had to achieve that goal. Even in the spring semester, my focus was on staying in shape and keeping my grades up and spending time with my girlfriend, who I saw every day. I also did summer school every year, with the idea being that I could graduate in three and a half years instead of the full four. I barely went out to social events, didn't really party at all, nothing like that. Also, admittedly, there was that intimidation factor. Like I've said, and like Laurie said, there was a deep sense of insecurity about my place there. I just assumed that everyone there was smarter than me. I was a football player and nothing more, and people would laugh at me for trying. How happy I was to be proved wrong.

Honestly, it wasn't until after I'd retired from the NFL that I looked back and realized I'd been fine there and that I fit in better than I'd thought. And yes, I ended up graduating early. Why? Because I set my mind to it. I identified it as a goal and went after that goal with everything I had. One of the best schools in the country, and I took less than four years to do it. Of course I was worthy. Of course I belonged. I just didn't accept it at the time, which is a shame.

So yeah, if I had to do it over again, I'd have made a better effort to get to know my classmates. That's the one hole in what was otherwise a pretty great experience.

But like I've already said, I did make some progress talking to others because I wanted to graduate and I knew I couldn't do it alone. Even when other students were generous and friendly, I'd hold back a bit, which worked against me a little but at least allowed me to get the job done. I did it out of necessity while still falsely thinking I wasn't on the same level as them. When I was on the football field, I was The Man. When I was off the field, I was just another guy.

Still, it once again hammered home the importance of being able to ask for help when you need it. Laurie helped me with that a great deal, and so did Isis, but I still had a long way to go. At the same time, though, there is something else I took from this, even though I didn't learn the lesson until years later.

That is, if you reach out to someone who thinks they're better than you and they laugh at you, there are two responses that are appropriate. The first is to realize that they are not worth a damn, and the second is to simply say, "To hell with them." Having the courage and the wherewithal to be able to say, "I need somebody to help me," is far more important than the embarrassment or humiliation that might come with the asking. And, one more time, there shouldn't be any embarrassment or humiliation in asking. If anything, there should be a sense of pride and accomplishment for having the strength to reach out. I don't think I can say that enough.

By the time I got to my senior season, it was the fall of 2013, and I was almost done with college. It was my final semester, both on the field and off. I was getting some calls about the NFL, and some people had asked me a few months earlier if I'd had any interest in leaving school after my junior year to go into the draft, but I knew that if I left, I'd never come back to get my degree. So I took out an insurance policy on my health, literally bought insurance on myself, came back for the final semester, and had my best season. I led the SEC in passes defended, with fifteen, and finished in the top ten in interceptions, with three. For the second straight year, I was named second team All-SEC and by all accounts was considered a serious prospect.

This shows you how far you can come if you stick with it, work hard, believe in yourself, and be strong enough to ask others for help and guidance. Three years earlier, I'd been thinking about quitting, but now I was about to graduate from a top school with a real shot at an NFL career ahead. I was one of the best cornerbacks in arguably the best football conference in the country, so I felt good about my chances. I finished my classes in December, and even though I walked with my class in the spring of 2014, I had essentially already graduated. I got hurt in the final game of the season but was back in time for the BBVA Compass Bowl in Birmingham, Alabama. We played the University of Houston on New Year's Eve, beat them 41–24, and just like that, my time in college was over. Come January, I was heading to Pensacola, Florida, to start training for the Combine, where college athletes gather to run drills and be judged by NFL scouts and general managers, held in March in Indianapolis.

I walked off that field having just played the final game of my college career, and the only thing that was on my mind was, "It's NFL time." I was fully focused, all in.

My life was about to change again.

CHAPTER 7

After Cancer

I closed chapter five with the idea that I had just gone through something that would lead me to walk away from the only life I've ever known, and now I'm going to start this chapter by building on that statement. What I'm about to say may sound a little nuts, but it is absolutely, 100 percent totally true: if I hadn't had cancer, I never would have retired when I did.

I have been talking for a while now about the level of confidence I had on the football field, a confidence instilled in me at a very young age by my dad and bolstered by my natural abilities. But that confidence hadn't always crossed over into other aspects of my life. For prime evidence, just look at the last chapter about my time at Vanderbilt and my reluctance to talk to other students for fear that I wasn't on the same level as them.

But beating cancer changed everything for me. It gave me more confidence in myself in every aspect of my life, including the football field. At first, each time I went out on the field, I thought, "I can't be touched right now. I beat cancer, I'm about to come out here and play my butt off, and there's nothing anyone can do to touch me, much less stop me." Sure enough, in the half season after I recovered, a season no one thought I'd be able to play in at all, I had three interceptions.

On top of that, while I'd always had a positive attitude, which had been a big part of how I beat cancer in the first place, that also was amplified. I told everybody who would listen—all the people who were around me at the time, friends, family, teammates—about the power of positivity, how important it is to life. I've never understood people who don't believe it, really, because it has always been so import-ant to me. I wasn't the biggest guy, I wasn't the fastest guy, I wasn't the strongest guy, but I have something that put me ahead of people because I worked my butt off and I believed in myself and I just made sure I would do whatever it took to get to where I needed to go. With football, I made sure I did what I had to do to make it to the NFL. It was the same with cancer. And now that I was healed and healthy, I knew it was something I had to do in the other areas of my life as well.

Beating cancer and looking over my career in the NFL and what I'd accomplished gave me the confidence to do what I wanted to do. More than that, it gave me the *right* to do it. It gave me the right to say, "Okay, I can stop doing this now if I want. I can do pretty much whatever I choose to do. I have earned that right." I had earned that right, and suddenly

I was in a place where I could understand the choices I had. I understood them in a way I never had before—that whatever I wanted to do, I could do. There was a spiritual meaning in that knowledge too, which I'll get into shortly, but more than anything else, the cancer ordeal led me to believe that I was worthy and I had the ability to do anything.

It is common for people to get depressed after they finish cancer treatments. They finish their battle and deal with all kinds of conflicting emotions, like anger about having had cancer in the first place or confusion about how others don't understand the stress they were under or any number of other things. But I had none of those issues. Pretty much the opposite, in fact, because all I felt was *great*. I was more confident in myself that my choices had healed me, and I had more faith in myself too. I trusted myself more. On top of that, it steered me toward the realization that I could be done with football, that I could make money another way. That I could become something else. Because if I could beat cancer and beat it in a month, then, once again, *I could do anything*.

Very suddenly, I had the notion that with discipline, intelligence, and yes, hard work, there was no telling what I could do with my life. I knew I could be whatever I wanted to be. I could go back to school, I could experiment, I could explore other aspects of life I'd never even considered. Until now. I knew I had the work ethic, and as we've discussed, that's half the battle. With that kind of discipline, setting my mind to learning a new trade couldn't be that hard. At least, it couldn't be as hard as I'd always allowed myself to think it could be. The point was, if I was willing to put in the effort, then I knew I'd be able to complete any task and overcome any challenge that may come up.

Again, this lesson doesn't just relate to me. It relates to anyone out there, anyone reading this, anyone who comes to any kind of crossroads in their life. As difficult as it might seem, conquering any adversity or overcoming any odds or solving any problem is all about being able to set your mind to it and having enough confidence in yourself to make the leap. Strike out. Move forward. Anyone can make this leap. You don't have to be a professional athlete—all you have to be is willing, ready, and totally focused on achieving your mission and realizing your dreams.

I will certainly admit to having certain advantages—mainly the freedom that comes with having significant financial resources—but I worked extremely hard to achieve those advantages. I don't think I need to apologize for the fact that, at my own personal crossroads, I had options. I paid for those options with blood and sweat and more than a little personal struggle. I earned them.

So even as I played through the second half of the 2018 season while trying to figure out what I wanted and how I was going to move forward, I was already making mental, emotional, and spiritual changes that would allow me to walk away when the time came.

For one thing, I found a new kind of spirituality that I hadn't really ever known before. My mom, as she pointed out herself, has a deep Christian faith, and when I was growing up, I would attend church with her. But while I never officially rejected that faith—that would be too harsh—I did walk away from it. That kind of devotion to religion never did anything for me, and I basically turned my back on it. Since then, I had never put much thought into any kind of spirituality or what it meant or entailed, but going through this personal crisis, even on a limited basis, made me rethink things a bit. Look at the world around me a little differently.

I didn't suddenly embrace Jesus Christ, like I imagine some others might, but I did start to have a better notion of my place in the world. I found that what made me embrace this idea and get in closer touch with what spirituality meant to me was a new thirst for knowledge. Having done so much research into the best ways to fight cancer made me want to know more about, well, everything. It almost felt like an unquenchable thirst. It was this new, driving desire to know more, to learn more, to enhance my education, even while I was getting that education. It was a desire to learn more about myself and the world around me on every single level.

I wanted to know things. Even though I had a college education and a degree from a top school, I still felt ignorant, in a sense, and I didn't want to be that way anymore. I wanted to be in a place where if someone told me something, I didn't just agree or automatically accept it as fact, but I wanted to actually educate myself on the subject—any subject—so that I could respond intelligently and from a place of solid, absolute knowledge. Like I did with the doctors treating me, I was into doing research, and through that reading and learning, I found a oneness with the universe that I equated to a new spirituality. By opening my mind to a different way of thinking, thinking outside the box, all the reading I'd done, all the research—it gave me a new level of peace.

There are lots of books out there about spirituality—more than any one person can read—but some of the ones I've read have suggested that the best way into religion is to take something from several of them. The stuff that works for you and helps to define your world view and guides you down the right path of morality and ethics. Sort of like a buffet. I like this idea and definitely subscribe to it, but that only works if you actually put in some time and learn about different religions and disciplines. That takes energy and interest and isn't the kind of thing you can do halfway. All of a sudden, I was finding time to do just that, and with the learning came fulfillment. It was a unique experience that I found myself thoroughly enjoying, to the point where I sort of couldn't get enough of it.

I had never thought of myself as ignorant before, but that's exactly what I was. I didn't know enough to offer my input on something, and I wanted to change that, so that's what I set out to do. It had worked with the cancer treatment, so why couldn't it work with, well, everything else? Again, this goes for everyone. Learn everything you can, absorb as much as you are able to, compare and contrast as much as you can so you can be a more active, engaged participant in your own life. If you're sick, it's your body, so you need to be aware of and involved in the conversation about how to fix it, especially since what worked for someone else might not necessarily work for you.

If you're at a professional crossroads, take charge of where you are and discover (or at least explore) what you want and what will fulfill you. If you're in a relationship that isn't working or isn't making you happy, take a deeper dive into the nature of what's causing the imbalance. Really try to figure out what will make you happy, then go after it. All of this stuff is intertwined, and it all comes back to the seeking of knowledge and truth and having a spiritual connection to that quest.

When I came to my personal fork in the road, I knew enough to stop and take stock. Had I not beaten cancer, there is no doubt in my mind I would still be playing football. If that hadn't happened, if I'd never been sick and had just gone through the 2018 preseason and regular season as normal, I'd have buried my dad and then kept on the same path I was on because there's no way I would have had the confidence in myself and my ability to walk away and try something new. I know this as well as I know anything: that I'd still be playing, that I'd be miserable for reasons I wouldn't understand, and that you would not be reading this book.

If I hadn't gone through it, I might have stopped to think about why I no longer felt the same connection to the game, and I might even have put it together that it had vanished with my dad. But there's just no way I would have believed in myself enough to be able to take that step into the void, nor could I have conceived that I might be able to have a life away from football. As I hope has become totally clear, the confidence I had on the field still hadn't completely transferred over into real life. This momentous event, the fighting and beating of a potentially lethal disease, was the first step in that process, one that has continued well past my actual retirement.

I certainly hope that we all don't need such a life-changing event to be able to understand ourselves better, but I know for a fact that this is what did it for me. I was lucky in a couple ways. One of them was the severity—or, I should say, the lack of severity—of my cancer; another was in my realization of what I was missing and how I could fix it.

I haven't talked yet about when I began meditating—that will actually come very soon, when I start getting into the nitty-gritty of my years in the NFL—but having begun the practice, I found it very helpful at this time. People think it's about stillness, about calming yourself, but meditation is actually more about organizing your thoughts than anything else. It's about taking a moment, embracing a quietness, and putting things together in your mind. It was a valuable tool while I was playing, and again I'll get into that, but it became an even more valuable tool while I was going through this process, as well as later when I faced the decision about retirement and my future (and yes, I'll return to that soon enough as well).

The act of meditating helped me focus on getting to know myself better and learning to understand that I had to do more for myself, that the ultimate trajectory of my life was up to me to determine and no one else. I had to be better, not just physically but mentally and spiritually too. When I was sick, I was confused about what was happening and why it was happening, and God, or whatever your idea of God is, was nowhere near me at that moment. So I needed to find my own path to what my idea of that was. Learning how to fight the disease, as well as how to move forward in my life, filled that hole. For what I think was probably the first time in my life, I stopped focusing on the external and started focusing on the internal. And we all know that true and effective change and transformation begins from the inside out, rather than from the outside in.

What I'm saying here is that there is an intrinsic power within all of us to help guide us down the right path, as long as we know and trust ourselves well enough to tap into that power and to follow that path. This, I found, was what helped me so much as I dealt with this illness and everything that went with it. Getting to know myself better led me to a sort of salvation, and it guided me toward what would be the road to real happiness and fulfillment in a way that football never fully provided.

I found that when I meditated, the ability to let my mind wander actually allowed it to focus. Doing that made me think more about what I was capable of and why I'd been holding myself back. I've mentioned before that if you tell someone they're great enough times, they'll start to believe it. Well, the same goes for when you say it to yourself. I started training my mind to think that I was different, that I was better than what I thought I was, and I kept doing it until it became second nature. I didn't accept being sick, and I got better, so the same could be true for anything else. I wanted to make a change, so I was going to do that.

Another thing I did was to stop bringing things into my life that would bring me down. I searched for things that were empowering and uplifting, like the book *The Four Agreements* by Don Miguel Ruiz, which offers great advice about how to live your life. The four agreements are as follows: don't take anything personally, always try your best, be impeccable with your words, and never make assumptions. It immediately became one of my favorites. That's another thing people do, and which I had certainly done—let negativity take hold in their lives and hold them back. It's not just about fear of the unknown, that's natural, but more about allowing the external forces I mentioned to hold you back for one reason or another. When I made that realization, I made a decision to rid myself of the negative forces around me, and the change was enormous. It helped erase doubts and reinforce the belief that I could do anything as long as I worked hard enough at it. It's important to remember that negative energy is *real*. It carries its own weight, and once you rid yourself of that weight, you create room for other things—positive, powerful, and life-affirming things—to come in. But both the decision and the follow-up action belong to you and you alone.

Sometimes it's as simple as writing down words of affirmation you can put on your mirror. Little sayings that remind you how good you are, how strong you are, how attainable your goals can be. It might sound silly, but seeing those sayings every day, first thing in the morning, looking back at me from the mirror, they helped. Repeated again and again, they took hold in my mind, improved my attitude, and eventually contributed to the positive changes I was making in my life.

So when I talk about my new spirituality, that's what I mean. This confidence, this belief in myself, this understanding of the power within me, it's something that's in all of us if we take the time and make the effort to really look and find it.

If you're wondering how my new form of spirituality is different from, say, my mom's, I think it's pretty simple. In lots of cultures, people believe in God and that He will do everything for them. I do the opposite. I no longer wait for anything and instead try to charge forward. I think the best way to boil it down is that their version is passive and mine is active. I have no interest in sitting back and hoping that God will do something for me when I can step up and do it for myself. This thought process began while I was dealing with the cancer, and it stuck. Honestly, I think that that change in thinking can help a lot of people push through their own troubles. I would never tell my mother, or anyone else for that matter, that they were *wrong* in their faith, but I know what works for me, and I know how well it has worked for me, and I'll take my version every time.

Don't get me wrong, this is really only successful if the same general rules apply. "Do unto others as you would have them do unto you," works pretty well and is something to live by. Another is, "Don't be a jerk." As guiding principles go, it's hard to disagree with either of those.

If you're wondering, my mom and I have not had any kind of conversation about this because there doesn't seem to be much point to it. I've never come out and told her I don't believe what she believes, and I have no reason to think she has any kind of problem with that. She certainly has never said anything about it, nor do I expect her to, because she respects me as a man, free to make my own choices. If she did, I would be very careful about it because I wouldn't want anything to change in our relationship, but I would certainly explain how I think, why I think it, and what it's done for me. Honestly, I think if we all took a moment to examine that in ourselves and respect that others might disagree, the world would probably be a better place.

That said, my life is infinitely better, fuller, and more meaningful now that I have a better hold on it and am a more active participant.

Since I'm on the subject of philosophy, I'll take this one step further and say that I believe what I've been talking about is actually one of the secrets to life. That is, putting work into whatever you want to do and going out to get it rather than just sitting back, being lazy, and hoping something comes to you. Make stuff happen.

Here, I'll say it again but louder this time: make stuff happen.

There are lots of guys out there who are faster than me, stronger than me, more talented than me, who never made it to the NFL, much less played there for five years and left on their own terms. Maybe some of them had bad luck, injuries, or faced other circumstances, but most of them didn't make it because they didn't want it enough, didn't work hard enough, weren't dedicated or disciplined enough, and that's on them. They were given the opportunity to be great and didn't take it. I never in my life wanted to think that way of myself, that I could let those opportunities pass me by—even though at least once or twice I almost did—and since I had my awakening, I never will again.

That's the thing that I think not enough people realize: We always have the choice. How we see the world, how we decide to interact in its midst, how we gain the energy to go after what we want, all of that is a choice. It's almost always in our hands. The question is, what do we do with it?

But Andre, you might ask, are you saying you never have any doubts anymore? No, no, of course not. I'm not a robot. When doubts sneak in, though, I simply seek more knowledge. The Bible says, "Seek, and you shall find," and when doubt comes into my life, I ask who has done this, who has gone through it, and how did they overcome it? I will go look for people who are actually facing what I'm facing, who have endured what I must now endure, or who have walked the path I'm about to walk myself, and I seek my answers there. Knowledge is power. And knowledge brings about enlightenment.

That's the other thing worth repeating: we can't do this alone. I certainly can't, and I'm going to go out on a limb and guess that you can't either. Sometimes our biggest hurdle is our own ego. I think I've shown that several times up to now, and this was a perfect example of it. If I am having trouble with something and then I see someone else do it, it makes it easier for me to do it as well. They provide me with guidance along this path because life has made it clear to me, again and again, that I can't do it alone. Sometimes it's talking to someone who has gone through it, sometimes it's reading a book, sometimes it's as simple as watching a video, but inevitably, it's there, waiting to be found, as long as I'm willing to look for it.

You can probably tell by now that I'm not a big fan of winging it. I'm going to look into things. Explore the possibilities. Weigh the options. I'm going to either plan for it or make a plan for it. I'm going to work out exactly the best way to do this. And then I'm going to execute it that way rather than saying, "Hey, you know what? Um, let's take it as it comes." Not my style. At all.

One of my favorite quotes is from Benjamin Franklin, who said, "If you fail to plan, you are planning to fail!" Smart stuff. Very wise. Words to live by. I certainly try to. By planning, by working it out, by being intentional about the path I set for myself, I am constantly betting on myself, just like you can.

It actually sometimes leads to frustration for me because I work so hard to enhance myself and learn and grow and develop, and when I see other people not doing that or taking the easy way out, it makes me angry. Like they're wasting opportunities.

What it comes down to is that I want others to feel like I do, in that I want them to learn new things. More than that, I want them to *want* to learn new things. Open your mind. Be different. Be better. Engage and explore the options around you, and if those options aren't there, *create* them. Don't let yourself become complacent. Plan for the long haul. No, I don't want to work my whole life, but by working my butt off now, I won't have to because even if it's more difficult at the moment, it'll be that much easier later. That's the key. It's part of the secret to the whole thing. It's clear to me that not enough people get that. They go for the quick fix or the simple solution that rarely works out, and it's just a damn shame.

Just so we're clear, I'm not talking about procrastination. That's something we all do, and there's no avoiding it. I'm talking about actually *doing*. I can put something off here and there as long as I know it's eventually going to get done. That's the difference.

I said before that I'd earned my retirement. That I'd worked hard enough and understood myself well enough that I was able to walk away, and that came directly from the fact that I had learned enough to do that. By making an effort to improve in the wake of a bout with cancer, I now had *the right* to walk away from what I'd been doing for my whole life, and it gave me *the right* to take control of my own life.

Taking it to the next step, it might even be fair to say that cancer was the best thing that ever happened to me because without it, I would never have found the courage to live the life I want to live. The right life for me. I don't regret what I went through, as I wouldn't have had the awakening any other way. It was difficult, it was agonizing, but I got there, and now that I'm here, I wouldn't change any of it.

Just in case I haven't made it as evident as humanly possible, I'll say it one more time. There's an important lesson to be learned here. The question you have to ask yourself is, "Do I have any interest in learning it?"

If your answer is "yes," then go after it.

Learn everything you can.

CHAPTER 8

Making the Team

A few days after I walked off a football field for the last time as a college student, I signed with my agent, Tony Paige, and then went down to Florida to start training for the draft. People started telling me I was probably going to go in the third round. Maybe even the second.

It didn't work out that way, of course, but let's come back to that.

Now that I had an agent, he sent me to EXOS Athletes' Performance Institute in Pensacola, where I worked out constantly to get into shape for the NFL Combine, to be held for a week starting February 19. This gave me roughly six weeks to get ready. They put me up in a condo (I had a roommate, Louis Young from Georgia Tech, who went undrafted but ended up signing with Denver and played four seasons in the league), gave me a stipend of $500 per week, and pretty much all I did was work out. I had finished all my classes, had essentially graduated, though I would walk with my class in May and actually receive my degree then. But there was no reason for me to stay in Nashville, especially when something like Athletes' Performance was basically built for stuff like this.

I basically had one job: train every day. That's it. Get stronger, get faster, work on my body so that I was in the best shape of my life for the Combine. For those who don't know what the Combine is, it's a weeklong gathering of the best three or four hundred players in college football so the pro scouts, coaches, and executives can judge them and decide whether they want these players for their team. It's pretty much a meat market, where they poke and prod us, make us sit in meetings, sit down and interview us, then for a brief time put us through drills, make us run a forty-yard dash, see how many times we can bench press 225 pounds, and a few other things like the Wonderlic test, which is a fifty-question written test that measures cognitive ability. It's all sort of demeaning, actually, but it's a necessary evil because apparently years of playing college football isn't enough for the scouts, coaches, and executives to base a decision on whether they think you're a talented player.

Athletes' Performance wasn't just about working out my body either. We also had a DB coach come in to teach us more about pro systems and sets. New rules to learn, like the fact that you can't touch a receiver once he's five yards past the line of scrimmage in the NFL. How the pros do it differently from college. All of it was valuable. All of it helped me, especially when I got to the Combine.

Before that, though, I kept training, then took a small break to play in the East-West Shrine game, an all-star showcase game for seniors. I played well there and got some attention, but then I chose to skip another showcase, the Senior Bowl, because I was only invited after someone else dropped out. My attitude then was "Screw them. They didn't want me first? To hell with them." Which, in retrospect, was pretty dumb, but that's when I was still letting my ego run things.

My feeling was that I wasn't a second-tier player, so I didn't think I should be treated like one. As I mentioned before, I was second team All-SEC my junior and senior years, meaning I was one of the best cornerbacks in arguably the best conference in college football. And they were only inviting me because someone else dropped out? No thanks.

Why was this dumb? I mean, it should be pretty obvious that if you want to play in the NFL (or, for that matter, if you want to succeed at anything in any walk of life), you should take advantage of every opportunity given to you to prove yourself to the people making the decisions. Seems pretty simple, right? Totally straightforward? Of course it does. Because it's plain as day, and I blew it. I am absolutely convinced that this set me back professionally. While I was sitting at home during the week leading up to the Senior Bowl, then skipping the game, someone else who was invited when I passed it up was getting the playing time and attention I could've been getting for myself. They were moving up the draft board, while I was falling down it. Because I was a big shot. This is the perfect example of how *over*confidence can work to your detriment, which is why it's so important to establish a balance.

Big lesson here: don't let your ego be your enemy. There are going to be times when you're not going to want to do something because of pride or because of some silly, misguided principle, but don't let it come back to bite you on the ass. Make wise decisions, and try to avoid letting your ego get so large it weighs you down or even buries you.

My time at the Combine went fine. I was told I scored well on the Wonderlic test, though I didn't do as many reps on the 225-pound bench press as I would have liked. Also, I wanted to run a 4.3 or 4.4 second forty-yard dash but only ran a 4.5. Still, I thought I was doing okay with a bunch of informal meetings with various teams, until a coach from the Cincinnati Bengals staff pulled me aside and told me I was acting like a "robot."

A robot? Me? What did he mean? Turns out I *was* acting a part. I was saying and doing whatever it took to try to get people to like me, overly eager to give them the answers that I thought they wanted to hear rather than just being myself. I was too busy trying to make a good impression, and in the process, forgot to just impress them with my abilities and what I knew. I forgot to be myself. I said to the guy that I was trying to show my best self, and he straightened me out, telling me that what was more important was to show people my *real* self.

I think what happened was that they put so much emphasis on knowing your stuff and acting like you know more than you actually know, and that made me feel like I should pretend like I knew everything about any team I was meeting with. Let's just call it for what it was: I was fronting, and he called me out. They wanted you to play ball and learn, not to try to be all-knowing and perfect. I guess that's what I was doing, trying to be the perfect prospect.

The unfortunate thing about it is that I didn't hear this feedback until close to the end of the Combine, which meant I probably acted that way with everyone else and maybe hurt my draft prospects even further while I was at it.

From there, it was back to Nashville to get ready for the Vanderbilt Pro Day. That was the day a lot of the same scouts, coaches, and executives came to campus to run the Vandy players who were entering the draft through drills and stuff. There were nine or ten of us, and we all worked out and tried to impress representatives from all thirty teams. But since it was with my friends, I was more relaxed about it, and I think I probably performed better. Since it was on my home field, it was just like doing what I'd been doing for four years. No pressure there.

The other thing was, after I got that critique from the Bengals coach, I was also much more myself. I totally stopped worrying about making an impression and just focused on playing. It was another important lesson for me to learn. Trying to be someone you're not or trying to be anything other than yourself is always a mistake. I made several mistakes on the way to the NFL draft, obviously, but that was definitely a big one. The combination of several things affected my draft position, for sure, but I think pretending to be something and someone other than what I was might have been the biggest.

It's not a mistake I'd ever really made before that stretch of time. Never in my life had I pretended like that, and when

I did, people noticed. Maybe you're better at that kind of thing than I am, but it seems to me that it's never a good idea to be anything or anyone other than yourself. The thing is, even if you're good at pretending, at some point, people are going to see through it, so why bother? You want people to accept you for who you are. It was how I'd always lived my life before then, and things had always turned out pretty well, so of course the first time I did something different, something that wasn't natural to me, it backfired. I'm actually grateful to that coach for calling me out on it. It opened my eyes.

Once the Pro Day was finished, it was basically sitting around for two months, waiting for the draft. I hung out in Nashville with Isis as she finished her senior year, I kept working out, and I began giving serious thought to where I was going to end up. There are seven rounds in the draft, and people kept talking about "the third round," that this seemed like the best place for me. As I said before, some people even thought I might go earlier than that, possibly the second round. The latest I'd go, though, would be the fifth. No way anyone would take me after that.

The draft started on Thursday, May 8, at the Radio City Music Hall in New York City. I didn't go there for it because that's something only prospective first-round picks do, but I was still checking in on it from Nashville. Also, I was graduating that Friday. The second round came and went without my name being mentioned, and then, after I got my diploma, I went straight to the TV and watched the third round come and go, once again without my name being called.

Same with the fourth round.

And the fifth.

And then I started getting angry. I was with my mom in a hotel in Nashville, watching and waiting in front of the TV and getting more and more frustrated. People kept telling me it was going to happen, that someone was going to pick me, that it was going to be okay, but when it kept not happening, I was pissed off. I started thinking, *Screw football*, and, *I don't even want to play anymore anyway*. I thought the guys in the league didn't even know what talent was; that somehow these guys who weren't as good as me were already picked, and here I was, still waiting.

Finally, I just left, walked around the hotel, wondering why and how this had happened and what I was going to do now that I wasn't actually going to play pro football. My mom tried talking to me, but it didn't help because I wasn't in the mood to hear it. Eventually, even though I was feeling low and sulking, I went back to the hotel room and people kept trying to reassure me, but now the seventh round was about to start, and things were looking grim.

But then, finally, the magic happened. On Saturday, May 10, with the first pick of the seventh round, number 216 overall, the Houston Texans chose me. I was relieved, obviously, and happy that now I was on a team and had the chance to actually fight for a spot on the roster, but I was still pretty angry. Rick Smith, who was the Texans' GM at the time, called me up and we talked. I was thankful, told him I was ready to get on the field and play, but I couldn't believe I'd fallen that far, that so many guys who I thought weren't as good as me had still gone before I did.

On the bright side, it renewed the chip on my shoulder, that I had to prove myself all over again. I had gotten cocky, thinking I was going to go higher than I was, and then I was knocked down a few pegs when I didn't go until the seventh round, but now I had to prove that I belonged. I had to show the team that had waited so long to pick me that they needed me. That I was better than some of the guys who they chose ahead of me and that, unlike most players who are picked as late as I was, I could stick around and make the team.

Someone once asked me if I ever talked to the GM or the coaches about why they waited so long to take me, but I never did. Once I was there, I guess it didn't matter why. They chose me when they chose me, and that's all that mattered.

Would I have gone higher than I did if I'd gone to the Senior Bowl? Or if I'd been more myself at the Combine? Or any number of other factors? Again, I think it doesn't matter because it worked out. If I'd gone higher, I probably would've ended up on a different team, and while I'd have been paid more money when I signed my first contract, I don't know that my drive would have been the same. I certainly wouldn't have felt the same need to prove myself like I did, so, in the end, it was a good thing.

The draft was later than usual (it normally happens in the second half of April), so there was less time between the draft and the first round of OTAs. There was a going-away party for me in Port Allen, where I thanked everyone for their support, then pledged that I was going to do something most seventh-round picks didn't do: I was going to make the team and stay on it.

So I went down to Houston and started working on that. As soon as I arrived and they gave me the team's playbook, I studied it like it was a final exam. Which, in a sense, it was.

I wanted to be the guy who knew the system better than anyone else. I had taken this personally as a slight against me, and so if I showed them I was better and smarter and more prepared, then it would be impossible to lose me.

First, though, there was the challenge of those first professional OTAs. Just as I had my freshman year at Vanderbilt, I wondered if I was in over my head. Because it was a rookie minicamp, I was doing every rep, which made me exhausted, and I got beat a couple times because my technique was off, and I started thinking, "Man, I don't know about this." When the veterans started showing up, it wasn't as hard, but I knew it was still going to be tough.

But then that's kind of how life is, basically. Once you jump into something, the first realization is how difficult it is going to be, "Wow, this is tough!" Then you get into it, and you find your way through it and eventually establish a groove and realize you're capable of it. Just because something is hard at the beginning doesn't mean you should walk away from it. Exactly the opposite, in fact. You make it through the tough part at the start, and then it'll get easier. When something is new to you, you just don't know what to expect. I didn't know what to expect. And then I finally kind of got the groove of it. I knew that just because I didn't have the hang of it right off the bat didn't mean I wasn't going to eventually nail it. Of course, that's where something like a good work ethic comes in. Get myself into a routine, and then I'd thrive. But in addition to having a strong work ethic, this requires patience. Be patient with yourself, but still demand excellence.

I had six weeks between the end of OTAs and the beginning of training camp, and when I showed up, I knew the system backward and forward. I was ready to impress everyone and show them what I knew and what I could do. The only problem was they weren't letting me on the field to do any of that.

When training camp started, I wasn't getting any reps, and that's a problem because reps are what you need to show what you can do. Reps, for those who don't know, are repetitions. Every practice play or drill is a rep, and the goal is to get first team reps because that means you're playing with and against starters. Well, as a rookie seventh-round draft pick, I was pretty low on the depth chart, so I had to find a way to get on the field and show what I could do.

There weren't many opportunities for me in camp, but once the preseason games started, things opened up a bit. The starters barely play in those games—or, at least, not in the first couple of them—because the team doesn't want them to get hurt, which gives players like me, players who need to show their stuff, a chance.

I know I mentioned this before, but it bears repeating: when you're given an opportunity, don't let it go by. Don't assume you'll get another one. There's no guarantee you ever will, so you'd better pounce on it when it's offered.

I know this because I pounced on mine.

I didn't get to play much in the first of the four preseason games, but in the second one, I had a pick six (that is, returning an interception for a touchdown). That was the team's first clue that they might have a real player on their hands, and once I showed them that, I started getting more playing time. With more time came more chances to make big plays, and that's what I did. It carried over to practice, too. In one rep, I was faced off against Andre Johnson, a star wide receiver coming to the end of what would be a fourteen-year career in the NFL. Andre was coming off two straight seasons of at least 109 catches and over 1,400 receiving yards, and he had led the league in receiving yards in 2012, with 1,598. Andre was a star, and while my rookie year ended up being his last year with the team (he went on to have one season in Indianapolis and a final one in Tennessee), he still would have eighty-five catches for 936 yards in 2014. So lining up against him, even in practice, was a big deal for me.

He ran a post route, and I was looking for it, so when I saw him take off and start running as fast as he could, I was right there with him, stride for stride, and then suddenly I was beating him. The ball came our way, I saw it headed toward us, and I jumped over his head and grabbed the ball on top of my helmet. Interception.

It was a big play; people whistled and cheered, and it was in that moment that I knew I could play in the league and that I would probably be fine. In fact, I think that was also the moment I solidified my spot on the team. Sure, I'd played well in the preseason games, but that was mostly against second- and third-tier talent, other guys just trying to make their own teams.

But this? This was me against one of the best in the league. A guy who finished his career with more than one thousand receptions, more than fourteen thousand yards, and is probably going to the Hall of Fame, and I played right with him. They knew then that I was for real.

I don't want it to be lost here that this was also big for me confidence-wise. Yeah, I've talked a lot about my confidence level on the field, but coming in as a seventh-round pick, already a bit behind the eight ball, that knocked me back a bit, and I found I had to prove myself all over again, not just to the Texans but to myself. After everything that had happened, even with the honors I got at Vandy, what if I wasn't as good as I thought I was? Or as good as people had told me I was? What if?

Having doubts is natural. I talked about this before. It's actually unnatural to *not* have them. The thing is, you just need to be able to conquer them. If you're good enough and believe in yourself enough, you can do just about anything. I think I needed the kick in the ass to remind myself that it wouldn't be the last time I'd get one (a kick in the ass, that is, but more about that in the next chapter).

The point was, I set out to show everyone that I was as good as a higher-round pick, and by making the team, that's exactly what I did. There were sixteen defensive backs in camp when it started, fighting for ten spots. I had begun at the bottom of the list, and slowly but surely, I climbed the ladder. Working as hard as I did meant the coaches noticed, and they weren't shy about letting me know where I was, which helped. One thing they told me was that, while I was impressive with the big plays I was making, they needed me to be more consistent. That was the difference, I think, between the college game and the pro game. The pro game is faster, and while you can get away with certain things in college—maybe having an off play or something—you really can't in the pros. Hearing that, I worked hard to get there.

Maybe one of the best lessons to learn here is that you have to be able to take constructive criticism. If I hadn't been able to do that, if I'd gotten defensive or thought I knew better than anyone or just felt like no one could tell me what to do, I don't know if I'd have made it. You'd be surprised how many guys don't make it because they can't hear criticism. Maybe because they never had to deal with it growing up because they were so good, but now that they're in the pros, they don't know how to handle it. I don't know about them, but I was not in a position to ignore it, so I worked with the coaches to give them just what they needed from me.

And then, suddenly, it's the last day of camp, the last day they're making cuts, and...no one came to talk to me. I saw people being called in to turn over their playbooks, I saw them getting cut, and I just wasn't. It started to hit me that, "Oh my God, I'm gonna make the team." I didn't know specifics, if I was going to be on the practice squad or on the main roster, but I'd made it.

I didn't really celebrate—it was more that I was just thankful. I had made an NFL team, and I definitely acknowledged it, but I already knew I wanted more. It was cool making the team, but I still wanted to be a starter. I wanted to accomplish something. I wanted to be a real playmaker. Someone valued. A genuine part of the team. I wanted security, and I knew there was still a good amount of struggle ahead of me to get it.

CHAPTER 9

Behind the Scenes

When you're playing in the NFL, making the team is only part of the battle. Once you're there, you have to prove that you actually belong, which is no picnic. It's grueling and exhausting and definitely rewarding but not without cost.

My first year I actually almost got cut. Once I'd made the team, I eased back on the throttle a little, which was a mistake because there was nothing ensuring I was going to stay. A lot of guys got hurt that season, but for the first few games, I spent most of the time on the sidelines watching. A few times I wasn't even activated on the roster for the game. I wasn't really taking things seriously because I wasn't playing, and so I wasn't paying attention in meetings and just wasn't working that hard. I wasn't giving it my all. I was sort of coasting.

As we got through the first half of the season, though, guys started getting hurt, and I began moving up the depth chart. Soon I was the third cornerback on the list, which meant that most of my playing time came in what's known as nickel coverage. It's called this because there are five defensive backs, instead of the normal four (and six DBs is known as the dime, which seems weird, but there you go).

Still, I wasn't getting many first team reps in practice and started mailing it in there too. As hard as I'd worked to make the team, I was reverting back to the same kind of behavior I'd shown when I first got to Vanderbilt and wasn't playing then either.

Things changed around the eighth game of the season when I found myself playing against the Philadelphia Eagles, a team that featured Jordan Matthews, one of my best friends from college. The Eagles also had Jeremy Maclin, who was one of the best receivers in the league, and Riley Cooper, so there was a fair amount of call for nickel defense, which was good because it meant more playing time but bad because I didn't do very much with it.

Several times I was lined up against Maclin, one-on-one, and I got lit up. Twice he beat me for big yardage catches, and I was just powerless to stop him. He made me look like a chump, like I wasn't even remotely prepared to face him. He had six catches for the game, for 158 yards, and two touchdowns. His longest play was for fifty-nine yards. That was against me. Then there was my buddy Jordan, who had three catches for forty yards and a touchdown, and that touchdown was against me too.

Remember what occurred in my first game as a starter in high school and how it led me to work my butt off to get better and how I'd vowed to never let it happen to me again? Well, raise your hand if you think I had the same reaction to that Eagles game (which, by the way, we lost 31–21). Is your hand raised? Good, because that's exactly what happened. I knew that another game like that and I might be gone. Later on, after I'd settled in, the coaches never directly confirmed my fears that I'd have been cut, but they didn't exactly dispute it either. They definitely told me a few times I needed to step it up, so I took that as proof that I was right. (At the very least, it makes for a better story.)

The point is, I knew I had to start bringing it, and that included practice. The coaches might not have expected the need to put me into the game, and that was on them, but the truth is that I knew better than to behave the way I was behaving. I knew better than to just go to practice, go through the motions, and not really learn what was going on or try to pick up the new schemes. I had been exposed for my poor play and for my lack of preparedness, so I started taking it more seriously, including being better prepared for the meetings for the team, the defense, and the defensive backfield, which I should have been doing from the start. As it turned out, the fact that I'd spent so much time learning the defense before training camp paid off because I'd already given myself a foundation to learn the new stuff. Before long, I was up on everything and knew the system as well as anyone. Probably even better.

Yes, there was a pattern to my behavior, and it wasn't pretty, but the lesson was still learned. Each time I was given another opportunity, which was great, and I absolutely recognize that not everyone is going to get that, but I did, and each time I made the most of it. I like to think the third time, in my rookie year, really stuck in a way that I didn't think I'd ever have to learn it again. So far that's the case, but I have to stay on my guard to make sure of it. Again, though, not everyone gets that second chance, so this is a case of, "Do as I say, not as I did." I was strong enough and fast enough in high school that I would have been given another opportunity eventually, but under different circumstances, I might have been shunted aside in both college and the pros and been out on my butt before I'd ever really shown anyone anything. That's why I know I was lucky and that I needed to take advantage of the second chance.

All in all, the shock of that one game gave me the push I needed, so I'm glad it happened, but I shouldn't have needed it at all. Once this mentality took hold, though, I was a solid player the rest of the season. I did intercept one pass, but that was erased because of a defensive penalty, which sucked, but that's the game for you.

Once I got through the season, I wasn't worried anymore about staying on the team because I knew I'd proved myself. The coaches were happy with my play, and I had brought my full effort to both practice and the games and had earned my spot on the roster. That didn't mean I let up on my work ethic or started coasting again, though. Just the opposite, in fact. I worked harder than ever to improve, and since the coaches saw this and understood I had certain abilities, they also saw an opportunity to fill a hole in the roster by asking me to switch positions. My whole life I had been a cornerback, but they wanted me to switch over to safety.

Before I get into that, though, a word about life in the NFL. There are TV programs now that show life in the preseason but not much that actually gets into the nitty-gritty of the regular season. The truth is, the day-to-day grind of it is sort of dull. The game is on Sunday, you come in Monday to look at film of the game, Tuesday you have off, and then Wednesday and Thursday you're alternately on the field and in meetings, talking about the upcoming game. And that's all day. Wednesdays and Thursdays are brutal, with full-contact practices and seemingly endless meetings. Friday is a lighter day, mostly just walking through everything, helmets and shoulder pads only. Saturday is more of the same, and if we have an away game, we'll travel for it, then Sunday is game day again. There's a lot of working out and lifting weights in there too. Nothing too wild about it. In fact, during most of it, you feel like a worker bee. A drone. Doesn't sound too glamorous, does it?

Anyway, coming back for my second season, the coaches pulled me aside and told me they wanted me to change my position. We had lost our top safety, D. J. Swearinger, who had moved on to Tampa Bay, as well as a couple other guys, and so when they asked if I'd be willing to try making a change, I said sure. It helped that I had worked so hard to know and understand the defense during my rookie year, so changing it up probably wasn't as hard for me.

Taking it a bit further, the setbacks that happened that pushed me to work harder ended up benefiting me in the long run. Pretty quickly I had gone from second-string cornerback to being in the mix to start at safety, and I wouldn't have been able to do that as seamlessly as I did without the knowledge I had worked so hard to accumulate. Like the previous times when something bad happened, I could have sulked about it or complained or allowed it to get me down, but each time I doubled down. In this case, the coaches saw it, recognized my effort, and rewarded me with the opportunity. I didn't need another one.

I don't think they expected me to start. I think they just wanted a backup because that year they signed Rahim Moore from the Broncos, who they thought would be a good safety, but since our system was different, he couldn't make it work. I guess in Denver he'd played one side of the field, but in our system, the safeties would switch off depending on the play or the coverage, and he just couldn't do that. When it became clear he wasn't getting it, I started getting on the field more. The other safety was another newly signed guy, Quintin Demps, who they signed in training camp, and he just fit right in. The two of us had great chemistry in the defensive backfield, and almost immediately things changed.

At first, before "Q Demps" came in, the starters were supposed to be Rahim and Eddie Pleasant, but neither was doing much in camp, and while I was doing well, the team didn't really trust me yet. Still, Rahim was one of the starters for the first few games of the season, alongside Q, even though he didn't love tackling people and mostly liked roaming around in the defensive backfield. But in the sixth game of the season, Q was hurt and I got in there against the Jaguars. I had two interceptions in the game, including the one pick six I had in the pros in a game we won 31–20. It was a big game for us because we were just 1-4 at the time, but that win turned things around. We won eight of the last eleven games that year and ended up winning the division, and it all started with that game, one of the best I ever had in the league.

The coaches responded pretty well to that. They basically said, "Whoa! We didn't know Dre could do that!" But still, they weren't confident enough in me to make me a starter, so the next game, against the Dolphins, we got killed 44-26, and Rahim was benched. That was it. From that point on, I was a starter. I got the opportunity to shine, and I did, while Rahim was often deactivated for games throughout the second half of the season, and by the end of the year, he was out of the league.

My background as a cornerback whose job was to cover the receivers came in really handy when I switched over to safety. A safety's job is different. The two of us work in the defensive backfield as, well, safeties, in case the receiver catches the ball or if the cornerback needs help against him. Usually, there is a strong safety and a free safety, with the strong safety usually playing closer to the line and favoring the "strong" side of the play (where the tight end lines up), while the free safety tends to be more of a roamer through the defensive backfield. But on our team, we went back and forth depending on the play. This was especially true when Q and I were playing together because our communication and chemistry were so good and we were both so versatile that it was easy to switch off. And because I had spent my whole life covering receivers, I knew how to read their routes better, and it was easier for me to recognize how a play was unfolding than a regular safety might.

So switching positions made my life in the league a lot better and, because I'd put in the work, much easier. I wanted to be better, both for me and the team. I wanted to reach the next level, and by making the switch and taking advantage of a unique opportunity, I was rewarded for it. This is good as a larger lesson too about the importance of staying resilient and flexible in what you do and how you go about your business. You'd be surprised how often having that attitude can work for you.

I had always fit in well in the locker room because I'm a pretty easygoing guy and I'm kind of quiet. I'm not terribly outgoing and am pretty good at keeping my own council. In football, and I guess in most professional sports, you're around these guys all the time, so it's better if you can get by without too much drama. I was sort of forced to step outside my comfort zone a bit, but that was ultimately fine because working with other top pros like them helps make you better. Especially when a guy is comfortable in his position and doesn't feel threatened.

Jonathan Joseph was that guy for me. He played cornerback for the Texans; he'd already been around for several years, and he made it easy to come talk to him about stuff. He would go out of his way to help you any way he could, and it was a lesson I learned and tried to put into action when I became established. He set a great example because, for him, it was all about winning. Whatever was best for the team was what he wanted, so if you came to him, he would be straight with you. Some guys, they would hold back on you, afraid you might be coming for their jobs. Not Jonathan. His attitude was that if we made each other better, we'd all be around for a lot longer. It was a much healthier attitude to have in the locker room.

Once you establish yourself as someone who's going to be there and stay there, the team treats you differently. Unless you're a first- or second-round pick, people aren't sure if you're going to stick around, so they don't go out of their way to know you. When it becomes clear you're not going to be someone who is in and out, they can open up. Again, I never really had a problem because I can generally fit in most places, but once I was established, they did take me in more. That also enabled me to be a better player because I got more respect from the team. More respect brings more confidence, so as I was getting better, people started to notice it. I was now one of the guys.

One other thing that helped me that second year was the practice of meditation. This, interestingly, became incredibly important to my future, but of course I didn't know that then. I just knew I needed help focusing, so I did an internet search on it, and it sounded cool. Once I started with it, I found that it was a really good fit. Meditation helped me center myself, helped me to settle my mind and my body, and helped me focus on what I needed to do and how I needed to do it.

It's not an enormous commitment either. Ten minutes every morning to steady myself and my thoughts, put them into some sense of order, and maybe explore some questions or issues that might be bothering me. I talked in the very first chapter about how meditation helped me come to the realization that I was ready to retire, and that's just the start. It obviously helped me with cancer, too, and of course, dealing with my dad's death. Having that quiet time to center myself, to achieve some sense of stillness, has become a pivotal and integral part of my daily routine. It also, I believe, made me a better player for those exact reasons. That's why I still do it every day right after I wake up.

Obviously, there is nothing still, quiet, or calming about football. Even when players are set before the snap, there is still a huge anticipation of what's about to happen. Receivers are in motion, defenders are moving forward toward the line of scrimmage or away from it, the offensive linemen who are supposed to be still are actually gearing up to hit somebody in a matter of seconds—and hit them hard. Football is a tightly coiled spring. A bomb ready to explode. You can't relax on a football field, can't unwind, can't take a moment to get yourself together.

But meditation is the opposite of that. It gives you those very things that you can't get anywhere else and allows you to get those same thoughts and feelings together so that you can, in fact, be more focused on the field. You can visualize things better, give yourself a better understanding of them. You can also take some time to figure out the best way to move forward in the face of tragedy or even explore how to more fully embrace your victories and triumphs. Once I found this practice and discovered it really worked well for me, it became indispensable.

Things really started to click my third year in the league. I never really had fun playing football, but the closest I ever got to it was in that third season. Meditation had me in a good headspace, I had established myself on the team, and the defensive backfield was the best one we had in the five years I was on the Texans. Q Demps was back, Jonathan Joseph of course, plus Kareem Jackson and Kevin Johnson, who was a first-round pick out of Wake Forest, and the five of us really meshed as a unit. Q was a big part of that; his personality brought everyone together, and we all pushed each other to be better.

It wasn't my best year statistically, but it was my best year in the league. Aside from the fact that it was such a good group of guys and that it was as close as I've ever come to having fun, it was the most productive and supportive atmosphere I've ever been around. The camaraderie was enormous, and there was also a drive to win, to excel. You'd be surprised how often that kind of thing *isn't* a part of an NFL team. To be in it, surrounded by it, to be involved with this attitude that excellence is attainable and every game is an opportunity, it pushes you more. Makes you work harder. I was involved, felt like I was a part of something special. Being around those guys, being a part of that unit on that team, did that for all of us, and we had one of the best defensive backfields in the league.

We once again won the division, then the first playoff game in the Wild Card round, beating the Oakland Raiders 27–14. The next week we lost to New England (the game where I intercepted Tom Brady) 34–16, and it was over. Q went off to play one more season in Chicago before he retired, and once he was gone, the attitude changed. He was the glue that held us together, and while Jonathan Joseph was still a great teammate and strong leader, his personality was different. It didn't feel the same.

The team wasn't the same either, as we had a terrible season, winning only four games, even though I had maybe my best season personally. I had seventy-one tackles, forty-seven of them solo, and three interceptions.

But something had happened before that season started that changed everything. During training camp, the team's GM, Rick Smith, came to me and said they wanted to give me a contract extension. Suddenly, I was in the big time. All the hard work had paid off before by getting me to the NFL, but now it was about to really pay off, literally.

By making me a millionaire.

CHAPTER 10

The Big Contract

I don't think anyone is ever really ready for their life to change completely. NFL rookie contracts are for four years, so I had no reason to think anything would be different going into the training camp for my fourth year in the league. But then Rick Smith called me in to tell me the team wanted to tear up the end of that contract and reward me with an extension, and suddenly, after all the years of hard work, of struggling and working and busting my butt doing everything I needed to do to succeed, I got the reward I'd been seeking.

When he first called me in, I was excited, but I didn't want to show that I was. I had worked my way up from a seventh-round pick to a starting safety and had played good football for three years. I had made an impact, was one of the leaders of the secondary, and the team had noticed. They saw how valuable I was, and they wanted to take care of me.

I was twenty-five years old and had really made something of myself.

The contract was three years for $15 million, half of which was guaranteed. It was an incredible show of confidence and belief in me and a clear way of showing that I was an important, valued member of the team. It made a difference in the locker room too. Money tends to do that.

I heard a story once about the Boston Celtics, back in the era when Paul Pierce and Kevin Garnett were leading the team, from 2007 to 2012 or so. Rajon Rondo was the point guard, and before the 2010 season, he signed a huge deal, five years for $55 million, and that contract won him a ton of respect in the locker room because that kind of thing matters. He had helped the team win an NBA title and was viewed at the time as one of the best point guards in the league, but it wasn't until he signed that deal that he really got acceptance on a different level from his teammates. It was the same in Houston. My contract wasn't anywhere near that large, obviously, but it was still significant. For other members of the team, it meant that I was established, that I wasn't going anywhere, and that, from a big-picture perspective within the team, I was worthy of respect.

Now I had earned respect with my play on the field and my attitude in the locker room, but this did bring it to another level. No matter how hard I had worked, I was still a seventh-round pick, so there was always that aspect of it in the backs of guys' heads. Almost like a subconscious thing. This new contract erased all of that. I had arrived, and there was no denying it. The way a pro player thinks is simple: "Oh, we know he's good, but the fact that the team thinks he's good too, that they're paying him, that means something. He made it."

That's what money does for you, and it's relevant, especially in a place as brutal as the NFL. When you're a higher-round draft pick, there's an automatic respect that comes with it because you get money right from the jump, so they assume you're really good. There's the downside of that, of course, that you have a lot to live up to, but I guess there's always some kind of hurdle you have to clear, no matter where you come from or how you got there.

But once the contract was signed and I had serious money and a firmly established place on the team, guys want to hang out with you more. It's weird, but as a beginner, I was cool with all the guys, the rookies, the veteran players, the people who have money, the people who didn't have money, everyone, just being who I was. I was never the guy outside looking in. Even going into my second year, people really liked me because I'm low key and don't cause any drama and was cool with everyone from the team's biggest star, J. J. Watt, to the last guy on the roster. I talked to everybody, so it wasn't that they suddenly liked me—it was more that I had been validated.

There was another aspect to this that I haven't really discussed yet but was actually a key part of my value to the team. Because I had worked so hard for so long to learn the system, I had become something of an additional coach on the field. There was extra pressure on me to not make mistakes, but that was worth it because they came to me and said, "You know the defense so well, so you have to make everybody great." I suddenly was given the responsibility of making sure other players knew their assignments, which wasn't really my job, but it helped make me even more valuable. It was suddenly on me to get everyone lined up in the right set and ensure that they all knew what the play was. This actually started in my third year, before I signed the contract, and maybe helped contribute to why they wanted to extend me. The added bonus of not just being a good player but also a smart one who could essentially do double duty on the field.

That first year of the new contract was the worst team we had during my five years there, which I mentioned toward the end of the last chapter. Like I said, with Quintin Demps gone to Chicago, the vibe was just different. There's also the fact that fifteen different guys got hurt, which didn't help. I mentioned that it was probably my best year statistically, but the thing to remember is that when a safety has a lot of tackles, it's because the other team is getting into the defensive backfield a lot. Big plays. In an ideal world, the safety has very few tackles. In 2017, I had seventy-one. The second-most I ever had was forty-eight. I'm no math wizard, but 50 percent more tackles seems like a lot. That should tell you something.

All of that was on the field and in the locker room. Of course, the contract had a big impact on my life outside the game too. Once you get money, more people come around asking for something. They feel like they have a right to take some of what's yours. Like sharks to blood, man, people come from everywhere looking for a piece of you, and you have to be able to say no.

Right away I took the attitude that I had made the money, and I'd made it for me. I'm willing to help you out, but I'm not ready to take care of the whole family as if I have a bottomless well of dough. That's also not really my style anyway. I'm generous, don't get me wrong, but I'm not a fool who will just keep handing it out and handing it out. That kind of guilt doesn't really work on me either. I think I covered this in the chapter about me and my dad, but it's worth repeating. Even when I signed my first contract in the NFL, the bonus was $65,000, and my family basically said, "Okay, we know you're a seventh-round pick, which means not that much money, so we're going to try not to ask for too much because we know you don't have it right now."

That made me angry. "Try not to ask for too much"? I'm willing to help out, sure, but people need to take responsibility for their own lives. This is the NFL. I'm not making money for you all to live like royalty. First of all, I'm not making nearly enough money to last forever if I keep spending it, and even then, at the time, I knew I wasn't going to play forever. The last thing I wanted was to be one of those guys who makes a bunch of money playing football, then retires and realizes he's wasted it all and is flat broke. That damn sure wasn't going to be me, and if that meant I had to say no to family and friends who came to me for money, then I was willing to be the bad guy who said no to them. Just as I'd worked hard to make it, I also recognized that I would need to plan for the future by being careful in the present.

Good lesson here too, since I'm talking about it. The impulse people often have when they get some money is to spend it because spending money is fun. Buying things is fun. Feeling like you can afford nice things or treat yourself to things you couldn't do before, all that is totally fun. I know fun is not a word I've used much in this story, but in this case, that's the best word for it. There is just no arguing it. Having money of any kind is fun.

But as much fun as you can have with that, the truth is, if you're not careful, if you don't plan, if you don't take care of it, that money is going to run out. Sometimes you can't help it because the money that comes in is barely enough to cover the important necessities, but when there's something more, instead of rushing out and buying yourself something nice, the smart thing to do is to put some of it away for the future. No one wants to work forever, and if that means going through some difficult times or working harder than you'd like so that it'll be easier later, that's a sacrifice it is always wise to make. Prudent too.

I like to think I've made that totally clear so far in the telling of my own story, but it's another thing I think is worth saying again. It's important. The younger you takes care of the older you. That's not just physically and emotionally true but financially too. I understood this, and when I signed the contract, the one big thing I bought was the house where I live now. But that's not a frivolous expense. That's a home, and it's equity, and unlike a car that loses value the moment you drive it off the lot, a house starts gaining value almost as soon as you buy it. Sure, there are varying aspects to it all—the real estate market is constantly fluctuating, for instance—but generally speaking, if you're smart about it, if you do your research and are fully aware of what you're getting into, you'll end up doing well.

I'll get to my experience in real estate soon enough, though. For now, let's stick with the money situation and how people started treating me differently since I had a lot of it.

That's another important thing to understand: no matter how much money you give somebody, they never get enough because they're not working for it, which is what happened.

At first, I had no problem giving people money. Interestingly, it was worse when I had my rookie contract because I didn't think much about the money I had and what I was doing with it. I only got really serious about what I was going to do with my money after I signed the bigger deal in 2017. During the first deal, I was giving people money, until at some point it hit me that this was not a good look for either of us, so I stopped. I had to point out that it wasn't just dumb for me, it wasn't terribly smart for anyone else either, because the day I left the NFL and was no longer making that kind of money, the money faucet would stop, and then where would they be?

My mom got it, and I still help her out regularly, but there are conditions, and she understands that. We set boundaries, and we don't cross them. Another good lesson. Boundaries are incredibly important. It's necessary to establish them, and then once they're established, you can't cross them.

For the first time, I was in a place where I could really plan for my future. The money I was making was not going to last me for the next sixty years, but I knew it was going to put me in a position to set me up for long-term security as long as I planned it carefully. It would buy me some freedoms, some security, and would allow me to have the wherewithal to figure out what my next move was going to be after football. I had been working for the money, but now I was going to get my money to work for me.

The first step in that direction was to learn more about money. How to handle it, the intricacies of it, how to make it last, all that stuff. I bought a bunch of different books on how to manage it. Suddenly, I had a million dollars in my account, and aside from buying my house, I just let it sit there while I figured out how to proceed. Once the season was over, I took the offseason to get my hands dirty and get into it all. *Rich Dad Poor Dad* by Robert Kiyosaki was the first book I read about money, and it was phenomenally helpful. It got me started in real estate, and pretty soon I'd purchased three rental properties, which now make me money every month. That was a smart move, and now I'm looking for apartment complexes. Good investments that bring in a return, as opposed to the money that I handed out to people that I was never getting back.

What are some of the things I learned? It might seem obvious, but one of the things I learned is that you have to educate yourself about every deal. Don't walk into something blindly or trust someone else's opinion. That's how a lot of people get screwed. They listen to others, fail to do their own due diligence, and their money goes bye-bye. The key is to do research. Figure out the pros and cons of the deal. Understand that you don't know everything, so try to find out all you can before you pull the trigger. Don't be afraid to ask questions. More importantly, don't think that asking questions makes you look weak. I learned the hard way that to ask questions about what you don't know is one of the most important things you can do. Educate yourself. Develop a thirst for knowing. Again, knowledge is power.

Also, be careful about letting someone else take care of your money. Yes, I know there are money managers and financial planners out there, and some of them are great. I'm talking about just handing the control of your finances entirely to someone else. The right move for me was to put myself in a position where I, and I alone, had complete control over my money.

I still feel like I don't even know enough yet, so I have to keep learning. We all do. I am constantly looking for different people to watch and learn from so I can have an upper hand. A lot of guys in the league get money and then lose it all because they don't know how to spend, save, and/or invest it properly. They don't understand money because they never had any, so once they get some, they just spend it like crazy because, what did we say before? Spending money is fun! And when you deal with a financial advisor, it's one thing to have him guide you and give advice on investments. It's another if you just hand that money over for this person to take care of everything for you. It's just robbery. You're paying this person's bills and paying them to take care of your money when you can do it on your own. You need to be in control of your own life and your own money, so you have to make sure you know what you're doing.

There's also the fact that you should know the difference between what you need and what you want. For instance, just because I suddenly had money didn't mean I was about to go out and buy a Lamborghini or crazy-expensive clothes I'm only going to wear once or anything that frivolous. I bought a house I love and a car that takes care of my needs, and that's it. I keep the rest of it pretty simple because that's what is going to make my money last.

Here's an incredibly simple lesson I've learned: don't spend more than you earn. Sounds easy, doesn't it? It's crazy to me that it even needs to be said, but…I mean, it does need to be said. Even with investments, it's important to have plenty left in the bank. You don't want to be in a situation where one bad investment wipes you out. I don't ever want to be poor again, and I'm pretty sure I won't be because I'm careful and I'm smart about my money.

The thing is, when it comes to money, it's often hard to be either of those—careful *or* smart. It only takes a little work, and as we've established, some people are just not willing to do that. I want to understand my money, I want to be disciplined about it, and I want to make more of it so that when I'm older, I won't have to worry.

Again, sounds pretty simple, right? But considering how many guys in the league go broke, it's apparently more complicated than one might think. And yet, it's why I was able to retire when I did. I could walk away because I had the money to do so. I had a cushion. The money I left on the table would have come in handy, sure, but since I was careful with what I had and smart about it, I didn't need the extra I left behind. Now I'm definitely worth a bit more than I was when I retired, and in time, I'll be worth a lot more.

You might wonder how it is that I came to this realization about how to deal with this newfound wealth. Part of it, certainly, was my lifetime of being a self-starter, but there was also the fact that I'd watched guys with huge contracts buying up all kinds of stuff or handing out lots of cash to the people hanging around them and then wondering where all their money went. There's the old Bible verse about a fool and his money soon being parted, right? Well, I am no fool. Seeing this happen right in front of me was all I needed to push me to learn and understand this stuff for myself.

The surest way to go broke is to never say no. Trying to please everybody? That's a direct road to the poorhouse. It's okay to say no, to say "I can't" or "I won't." A million dollars is a huge amount of money, but it's not enough to support five families forever. Or even one family. Being able to say no isn't selfish, it's self-preservation. Helping people is great, but it's got to be on your terms. Sometimes people don't want to hear that, but the most important thing is taking care of yourself. It's always nice to have a compassionate heart, but don't let it turn you into a human ATM.

I was already making some pretty good money those first three seasons. Being paid a few hundred thousand dollars a year allowed me to figure some stuff out before the big money started coming in. So it's not like all of a sudden I went from nothing to everything. Because of those first three years, the transition to bigger money was a far easier one than if I'd been handed a big contract right out of college. And transitions, after all, are sort of the point of this whole book.

I talked before about how much fun it is to spend money. Well, it's no fun at all to *learn* about how to spend it, how to save it, and how to make it work for you. It's actually sort of static and dry. But then, there's a lot of stuff in life that isn't fun but is necessary. We've spent a lot of pages talking about those things, and I would argue this is one of the most important because, in the long run, your understanding about money—how to get it, how to keep it, how to grow it—will allow you to make more.

So yes, sure, spending money is fun, but I'll let you in on a secret:

Making money is the most fun of all.

CHAPTER 11

The End of the Beginning

Walking off the field in Houston that January day, right after the upset loss to Indianapolis that would prove to be my final game, I wasn't totally sure at that moment that I'd actually played my last game. I knew leaving the stadium that day that I had a lot of thinking to do, but I also knew I needed to wind down. The whole year had been so stressful and difficult, the combination of fighting cancer, losing my dad, working my butt off to get back on the field, hurting my shoulder, then having to work hard to do it all again…it had all been way too much. By the time that playoff game ended, I was numb.

The first couple of days after that game, I was finally able to relax, take a breath, and figure out what was going on in my head. It was the first time I could sit and ask myself what my next move was. I knew I didn't like playing anymore, but I wasn't sure yet that I could stop doing it. Basically, I just knew I wasn't happy and had to examine that part of it and figure out a way to change that so I wasn't quite so miserable.

The good thing about having just gone through the cancer ordeal was that it had forced me to sit out a good chunk of the season and in the process think about the role of football in my life. Aside from that one year before high school, it had been the first time in almost twenty years that I hadn't been playing during the summer and into the fall, and the time away from it allowed me to see what life would be like without football and that my life wasn't just about the game. Football had been such an enormous part of my entire life; I had tied myself to it. It was who I was. It just seemed natural to think that my life wasn't much of anything without football. But fighting cancer gave me the chance to see what life was like without having to go to practice every day and without knowing what my Sundays were going to hold. The disease actually gave me the opportunity to explore parts of myself that I'd never explored before. Being off the field helped create the physical, mental, and spiritual space I needed to try on some new ideas, maybe explore a couple of new directions.

Football is not easy, of course, but it had always been pretty easy to me. Don't get me wrong, I worked incredibly hard to make the NFL and maintain my place there, but it was still just always a thing that I did. I understood the game, I knew my part of it, and I knew that I could do it well, and that made it a pretty simple thing for me. But I still felt trapped by it—as if I were just going through the motions—

and it got worse when the doctors and coaches issued orders that would keep me off the field. I wasn't free, and the longer it went on, the worse it felt. That sense of not being able to do what I wanted, not having control over my life, was frustrating and disorienting, which only added to the stress of everything else. Everyone wanted me to be better, but once I was, the coaching staff still held me out of games, which made me mentally worse. It was frustrating, but it gave me more to think about once the season had ended. I knew I was angry about it; I knew that I was leaning toward walking away because of it, but I also knew that I had to take some time to make sure I made the right decision. And I wanted to make this next decision from a place of knowledge rather than from a place of anger.

This is a great place to stop and talk about another important lesson: don't make rash decisions based on emotion when your life and career are on the line. Our natural instincts generally tend to be good, and I follow mine, for sure, but that doesn't mean I rush to judgment. I still understood that even though I was pissed off about how I had been handled, my anger wasn't enough to base an entire life decision on it. I think people do that too often: they let their emotions rule their rational, strategic thinking and end up making rash decisions that they later regret. Today I can comfortably say that I have established my own pattern in life and that I am not someone who wings it. I've always been a pretty careful planner, and if anything, that kind of intentional thinking has only become stronger since I retired from the NFL. If I had just decided on the spur of the moment that I was done with football—if I'd just walked off the field after my last game without thinking it through properly—I would have been making a decision that was based on emotion rather than on intellect. And I might have ended up regretting it. The trick is to not have regrets about major life decisions, and this involves doing the careful thinking and the internal due diligence to ensure you think things through clearly. No one else can do this for you. It's something you have to do on your own.

In this case, I was making the biggest decision of my life, so I knew it had to be a rational one. This was about my future, and I was only twenty-six years old. I was pissed off and kind of jacked up a bit about football, and before I did anything certain, I needed to ask myself, *Who am I?* Going through that process gave me the courage to find out, but you shouldn't have to fight cancer to be able to do that. You should be able to ask yourself that important question—and do whatever you need to do to find the answer—on your own.

I think the key is to ask yourself, "Is there more than this?" When I was held out of football, that was the first time I started to think, "Wait a minute. If I'm not playing football, what else is there for me? There *must* be something more than this." It was almost a preview as to what my life was going to be like once I walked away from the game. Looking back on it, I consider myself fortunate that I had the time and the interest to ask myself those questions.

So with that in mind, I set about figuring my next move, asking myself even more questions about what my life was going to look like. Would I be able to survive in the regular world? Could I do the nine-to-five thing? What would my interests and passions be? How could I set myself up financially to last for, oh, the next sixty or seventy years without ever getting another penny from playing football?

Luckily, I now had time to start figuring that out.

One of the things the NFL does for its players is create partnerships with other companies and organizations that provide players with externships to help adapt to life after football. I talked to my agent, Tony Paige, about it, and we looked into the right place for me to give it a try. Interestingly, the FBI is one of those places that works with the league, but that didn't interest me.

There was one that did, though. I already mentioned that I'd started meditating back in my second year in the league. I'd used a meditation app called Headspace, which had helped sharpen my focus both on the field and off. It had also helped me battle cancer for the same reason. As it happened, Headspace had a relationship with the NFL, and that felt like a perfect fit. The thing was, the program wasn't going to begin until the beginning of March, which meant I had a few weeks to kill before I went to Santa Monica, California, to work in the Headspace office.

I didn't want to go anywhere, I didn't really want to see anyone. I just wanted to sit with myself and get out of my own way. The idea of retiring was now in my head, and I was really wrestling with it, but it was still really scary, and I wasn't ready to fully dive in. There was actually part of me that wondered if people would even still like me if I didn't play football. I know, I know, that's nuts, but knowing it was nuts didn't mean I stopped thinking about it or that it wasn't weighing on me. If it were that easy to just shed your paranoia and insecurities, everyone would do it and we'd live in a nicer, more balanced, more compassionate world. But it's *not* that easy. I can look back now and understand that it's natural for someone in my position to worry that being a football player was the only interesting thing about them and also see how silly that worry really was. But being in the middle of it and being unsure, being in between things and not knowing what the best move really was, didn't feel so silly at the time. This, after all, was a serious decision.

I wanted to be more in tune with myself so I didn't have to worry about validation from other people. Playing football, I got so much validation from others. People were always saying, "Ah, you're so great, man! You're so great, Dre! I love you, man!" People love you because you play football. Part of me realizes now that they might have loved Number 29 the player more than they loved Andre Hal the man. So when I left the field, I was wondering, again, "Okay, who's cheering for me now? I'm in the house by myself, nobody is cheering for me here." The motivation to be someone else, the Dre that people thought of when they thought of me, was gone. Now I only had the motivation to be myself. I'm Andre. Dre is the public persona; Andre is who I really am.

So for the first couple weeks, I didn't do much. I kept working out but was doing it to stay in shape and for stress relief, not to keep myself right for the football field. I meditated a lot. I read a lot. Having done so much yoga while I was dealing with cancer the year before, I began doing a lot more of that too. Interestingly, in doing more yoga, I found some answers I didn't expect to find, which helped me a great deal.

In the course of doing a ton of yoga, I met Jaz Porter and Alicia Stephenson, who have an internet show called Yoga

Evolution TV. They asked me to come on as a guest while they practiced yoga with a group of about twenty or twenty-five people. While I was there on the show, I felt a new freedom. I was able to just let go, open up, and talk to people about my life. That's not something I normally do, as I'm super private, and the thing is, I didn't have any intention of doing that when I went there, but they were so open, so centered, and so cool, I sort of couldn't help it. I just opened up, and it carried over after we were done because it felt so good to do it.

One of the things that touched me about them was how much they loved their lives and how confident they were in themselves. I wanted the same thing, and while I'd gained some off-field confidence over the years, it was still on the field where I felt the most sure of myself. Obviously, I was floundering a bit off the field trying to figure my life out, but Jaz and Alicia reassured me that people were interested and that they wanted to hear my story. At first, I didn't believe it, but they saw in me a level of self-confidence that I didn't really see in myself. They didn't see me as just a football player. In fact, they didn't even know I *played* football. They only saw me as Andre, this interesting guy they'd met who practiced yoga.

That's when I realized, "Damn, I *am* more than a football player. I *can* be more than this." It seems simple that this is all it would take, but sometimes it's the simplest things that bring you face-to-face with the most powerful and profound knowledge. Two women I barely even knew helped bring me to this realization. It's another important lesson about people: that a little positive reinforcement can actually be transformative; it was for me, anyway. It went a long, long way. It also just goes to show that even someone like me, who might seem to have his act together, can be struggling underneath the surface.

I've said it before, but it always bears repeating: you shouldn't judge a person, for good or bad, until you've spent some time in their shoes. Or, if that's not possible, at least until you've spent some time getting to know them or understanding their particular situation. Before reading this, you might have taken one look at me, even as I was in the middle of my career, and thought I had it all and that I had the world by the tail. Obviously, you would have been wrong.

But now, getting into February of 2019, I was just finally starting to get my head around it all. Thanks to Jaz and Alicia, the idea of being taken seriously away from the football field wasn't so crazy or so scary. Neither was the idea that I might be a pretty cool guy myself.

It's funny the way the mind plays tricks on itself. I knew my friends and family loved me, but I still somehow tied it back to football. Now I had to go back to my old self and realize that people didn't just like me for playing football, they liked me for who I was and am. That experience, doing yoga, getting myself centered and focused, and something as small as two women who showed me that I was worthy without even knowing my connection to football, got me on the right track to understanding that I was going to be okay and that people were going to love me no matter what.

Eventually, it got to be March, and I went off to Santa Monica to work at Headspace. It was only a three-week program, but it did a few things for me. As I mentioned before, it showed me that I could exist in a traditional nine-to-five world without needing the constant action of the football field and the weight room.

Working at Headspace was an eye-opener for me in other ways too. For one thing, it showed me that people are all basically the same. I somehow expected people who weren't athletes to be different or, actually, that athletes were different from regular people. But the thing was, the conversations we had in the Headspace meeting room were pretty much the same as the ones we had in the Texans' locker room. On top of that, while working with the company's head of sports and fitness, Lindsay Shaffer, I was given different projects to see how meditation as a practice and a technique might be better integrated into the NFL to help its players. The fact that I used it in my own life was an added benefit, since I could speak to how much it aided me.

I loved the experience at Headspace. I loved every minute of it. The work, the people, all of it. I made friends I still have today, and it gave me insight about myself that was invaluable. I did things I never thought I'd be able to do, like my final presentation, which went much more deeply into how Headspace can work with the NFL to help players with meditation. Little things that can be big. One example is getting a team's star player to buy into the concept. That way he can bring the notion to the rest of the team in a way a coach can't. A coach is an authority figure. A star is one of us. It carries more sway. Other things were part of it too, like mindfulness training and how it can help performance. I even made a mock poster that I thought could be put around a facility—in training rooms, inside lockers, wherever, really— that had a mnemonic device I came up with: Mental Edge

Develops Impeccable Transformation Achievable Through Execution (spell it out, and you'll see how clever I am).

That presentation, though successful, was also incredibly hard for me. I'm not someone who enjoys getting up and speaking in front of others, but it was a requirement for the project. I had to get up in front of everyone and present my findings, but see, that's also part of the growth I was discovering. I was there with a legit project about meditation and how it affects guys not just in the NFL but also any other major sport, and the fact that it was so well received was another thing that helped me realize I could do whatever I want to do if I just put my mind to it.

In football, there's not a lot of talking. I didn't have to do anything but play, and play well. Sure, you have to perform in front of people, but it's different. You don't really *talk*. You aren't made to feel stupid if you flub a line. In football, you're just doing your thing, whereas in the real world, you have to speak and act and do things a certain way. I had never done that before, but now I found I could, and it was okay.

I finished the externship on March 25. Over the next week, I did nothing but get my thoughts together and wrap my head around the decision I was making. I knew what I wanted to do but was trying to figure out how to do it because it's hard to stand in front of people and tell them *I'm done*. I had to build up the courage to actually tell the people close to me about it, not to mention the team. I knew that some people were going to try to talk me out of it, that they were going to think I was still sick, any number of things, and I had to brace myself for all of it. I was finally confident enough to make the decision, stand by it, and know I was going to be okay, but I also knew that there was going to be a ton of pressure on me to change my mind.

The funny thing was, I think that if I'd been a big star, like Andre Johnson or J. J. Watt, I wouldn't have been able to retire. I know it sounds nuts, but I think guys like that can't just walk away because there's too much pressure on them, too many things and people depending on them. Injuries are one thing, but when you're that good and that big a star, the responsibilities are too great to be able to just walk away. I was a good player, a solid player, but certainly never a star. For me, while it wasn't exactly easy to walk away, it was certainly less hard than it would have been for someone better known than me. It's always harder for a big star to walk away from the game because you're so much more involved in it. For someone like me, again, it wasn't easy, but it wasn't nearly that hard either.

I'll go one further and say that, without naming any names or speaking for anyone else, there are plenty of guys in the NFL who play because they feel like they have to, not because they want to. Some guys need the money; some guys like the fame, but they don't love the game. There are lots of guys who do, don't get me wrong, but more than a few do it without that love. One of those guys, obviously, was me. Those guys stick around because they still need something. In the end, I didn't.

Transitioning from one part of life to another was only possible for me because of the things that yoga and meditation had given me. The ability to center myself, to focus, to get inside my own head, all helped me get to where I needed to be. I'll be honest, I wish I'd had someone else to talk to, a therapist or someone, because that would've made it a lot easier.

Actually, I'd like to take a moment to talk about that. I've mentioned previously that we shouldn't view certain things as weaknesses. Things like apologizing, taking responsibility, admitting when you don't know something, asking questions—all of these are necessary and important and should never be seen as anything other than essential parts of being a well-adapted adult.

I'll add another: being able to admit you need some help. Sometimes that's physical, sometimes it's psychological, and if I had to do this over again, I definitely would have gone to see a therapist of some kind. I would have liked to have talked to a person who could be objective, who was trained to listen, who could help me work through the things that I was trying to work through on my own. It's a small regret because it all worked out, but I think it would have sped up the process a lot and made it less painful. I was holding it in, and talking to a professional not only would have allowed me to get it out, it would have also allowed me to come to a conclusion a lot quicker. I can't recommend it enough for someone who might be at a similar crossroads.

There is a stigma attached to all of the things I've mentioned in the last couple paragraphs, but there shouldn't be. We should be able to get over ourselves and do these things because they can help us, but we don't because we're afraid it'll make us look weak or fragile. Or vulnerable. What they do, though, is make us stronger. More balanced. More human.

Something else that has a stigma attached to it is being able to admit when you're scared. I was terrified of walking away from the NFL, but overcoming my fear helped me understand that the decision was the right one. Fear has a way of preventing you from thinking clearly and rationally, but once you push through it, you can see things for what they really are.

On April 1, 2019, I called my mom and my sisters and told them I was retiring from football. They didn't believe me, of course, especially my mom, who thought I was just going through something. A phase or whatever. That I wasn't being serious. But I knew how serious I was. I knew how much I'd changed. A year earlier I couldn't have done this. That's how different I was in just twelve months. (Side note: after I'd been retired for a month, my mom finally accepted that I was done for good. We definitely have gotten closer after I retired and talk more often. When we do talk, it's much more about the things going on in my life than about football. She was also proud of me for making that decision on my own.)

The next day, of course, I made it official, and you know the rest of that part of it. But even though you now know most of my story, there's still quite a bit left to tell. Not necessarily about what's already happened but what was *about* to happen. I was about to take an enormous gamble on myself, and now that I was finally confident enough to do it, I was also confident that I'd be able to succeed. At the very least, I was ready to take the first step necessary to achieve that success.

CHAPTER 12

Business Lessons

S o we're clear, I had doubts.

The week or so after I announced my retirement, I sat in my house and wondered if I'd made the right decision. I needed to settle down. I was still in the moment, still kind of nervous. It took me at least a week to calm myself back down and feel normal again because I felt like I had just stopped my life. I'd just taken a big step. Maybe the biggest I'd ever taken. It took a while to sink in that I'd really made this choice. I knew I wanted it, but at the same time, a part of me also felt like I had made the biggest mistake of my life.

Did I really just stop playing football? Was that really what I wanted? I mean, of course it was, but since I wasn't used to *not* playing football, I had to wonder if I'd made the right move. I had been playing pretty much every year of my life for twenty years. I should have been getting ready to start up again, get into shape for the summer camps and the new season. Now I wasn't doing that, had no reason to do that, and I'll be honest: I felt lost. But then I just got my mind on other stuff. I should add here that I didn't just "get" my mind on other stuff, I *put* my mind on other stuff. I was deliberate and intentional about shifting my headspace, about getting my mind right again. There wasn't anything passive about it. I did a lot of yoga; I started working out again, boxing, mostly, because I needed a distraction and didn't know what else to do with myself. I wasn't working, I wasn't training for football, I wasn't doing my DB drills, so working out was a great option. It felt familiar, *and* it helped me with the transition out of football life and into real life.

The sense of freedom I'd initially felt before, when I'd left the Texans' facility on April 2, finally returned about a week later. But it still didn't feel like *full* freedom, if you know what I mean. The truth was, I didn't really know how to be free. Sure, I was working out and staying in shape, but it was a different kind of shape. It wasn't "game shape," it was just staying healthy. I was doing things that I'd always done, but now I was doing them just for me, and it was sort of hard to wrap my head around that. Even though I was only in my midtwenties, I needed to reconfigure everything in my life. Not an easy feat. And definitely not something that's going to happen overnight. In fact, I think it would be really surprising if it did. If you're ever in that situation and can just turn it on or turn it off like that, I envy you. That's damn impressive.

My process was pretty short, but still, there was that initial feeling of uncertainty, of being at loose ends. Working out, meditating, doing the yoga, eating right, all those things helped me to settle in, especially once it sunk in that I was now doing it only for myself and not for anyone else. Once that happened, I was able to take a look at everything else and begin to put together my plan for the rest of my life.

The first obstacle was boredom. Even working out twice a day left plenty of hours to kill. The good news was that buying my house had sparked a new interest: real estate. The woman who'd sold me my house, Rene West, had suggested I get my real estate license because it meant I could work my own deals, and, not only that, but if I orchestrated a purchase, I could also get a commission from the seller, even if I was the buyer. So I enrolled in school to get my real estate license, which took me about six weeks of immersive classes and tests. It was difficult, but I got it—I focused, did the work, and achieved the goal, which is pretty much my pattern—and in the process, I kept my mind occupied with something that really had me busy. You want a cure for boredom? Go back to school to get your real estate license. It's a great challenge, and it provided me with a new set of goals. Plus, I enjoyed learning new things. That's something I'd already come to know about myself.

Years after I'd graduated from college, I found that I actually liked school. I liked the classes and the structure, and as I've mentioned before, I'd rediscovered a love of learning and reading, so this new interest in real estate was sort of perfect for me. Getting back into school mode wasn't as hard as I thought it was going to be. In fact, it was kind of easy. It was just a question of getting used to sitting in a classroom and listening, focusing, paying attention. Truth was, it wasn't all that different from being on a football team, with all the meetings we had during the week and the films we watched and all the studying we had to do about the other team. In fact, I would say that helped me more than anything else, being used to meetings and sitting in a room studying and going over stuff with a bunch of other people. I would go so far as to say that when you come out of the NFL, that's the perfect time to go back to school because, in a sense, you never really left. Where else do you have that pattern of sitting in a room and studying like that? They're the perfect match when you think about it, and in school, there's no tackling. Which is a bonus.

That part didn't occur to me at the time, so when I found myself able to so easily switch back into student mode, it was comforting to me at a time when I needed it. The meditation helped, obviously, but honestly it was the combination of several things allowing me to push through, grind it out, and accomplish the goal. By the end of May, I had my real estate license.

While I was doing this, I was also looking for properties to buy. Since I'd decided that real estate was the way for me to get started in the business world, I wanted to find something that would immediately start to generate revenue. I found a town house I liked that I knew could be a good rental property, and it came together very quickly. The closing, in fact, was during one of my classes, so I had to run out during the lunch break, sign all the papers, take care of everything, and then get back before I missed too much. Closing the deal made me feel like I had accomplished something. Something I'd done entirely on my own. I'd bought my first house, but the rental property was different because it was a business decision. It made me happy. I'd done this all by myself.

Not that it wasn't without issues, though. After all, my loan hadn't been approved at the last minute, and I think it's important to talk about that, as it typifies the institutional racism that exists—and has always existed—in our country. I was a retired football player with millions of dollars and had more than a million dollars in various accounts in the bank. A quick aside: never have more in your account than is insured by the government. The Federal Deposit Insurance Commission insures the funds of an individual's bank account for people who have money in one of their member banks (which is most of them). Currently, any account with up to $250,000 is fully insured, which means that if something happens to the bank, if it fails or has solvency issues or whatever, the government will cover it. Anything more than that and you're screwed. So while I had more than a million dollars in that bank, it was spread around so that I wasn't exposed.

Still, despite the fact that I had more money *in the bank* than I needed for the loan, you would think that it wouldn't be a problem. But, see, it apparently doesn't work that way because the loan officer turned me down. He said that since I was retired, I had no regular income coming in, so he thought that the risk was too great. Never mind how much capital I actually possessed. I think he assumed that I would blow the money I'd made in the NFL and that eventually I would lose the property, so it wasn't a good investment for the bank.

I had been through this before when I was first drafted. I wanted to buy a car—a Dodge Challenger—but because

I had no credit, no one would give me a loan, and I ended up going to the Texas Credit Union Bank to get it. That time, since I'd never had any money, I hadn't been able to establish proper credit, but now, at the age of twenty-six, after having made millions and buying a car and a house and establishing equity and good credit, I still wasn't qualified for a $200,000 loan? A loan that was far less than my net worth? What kind of sense does that make?

Let's just say that if a White guy with a million dollars in the bank had retired and wanted a similar loan, I don't think that loan officer would've had the same concerns about how he would handle his money. They would probably give me money to buy a Bentley, but a rental property? Nope.

Anyway, two days before the closing I had to run around and find someone to give me the loan, and sure enough, the Texas Credit Union Bank came through for me again, and I closed the deal. Later in the summer, when I purchased two more town houses I would use as rental properties, I went back to the same place, but they said it was the last time they'd be able to do it, as they're a small bank and didn't want to overextend.

This problem won't come up again, not only because I have the money but also, more importantly, the three properties I own will serve as collateral for anything else I might buy. I have established great credit and good equity, and that will be stronger than any one person's judgment, regardless of what kind of power they might have in a particular bank. As a matter of fact, the same bank that turned me down later came back and offered me a $1,000,000 line of credit. I passed.

Now, because you need to not only have goals but also be able to execute those goals, I've updated my plan. The goal was to have two rental properties by the end of 2019, and I had three. Originally, my goal for 2020 was to have a multiunit complex, somewhere between four and ten units, but then the pandemic happened, and my goals shifted. Now the goal for the immediate future is just to find two more quality rental properties, regardless of size, to expand my portfolio. But I'm not just going to buy something because I need to fulfill the goal—I will only buy it if it's the right fit, the right circumstance, the right price. This, while I'm also in business school, getting my MBA, but more about that in the next chapter.

Let's go back for a moment to the loan I didn't get. My initial reaction to it was to just walk away and forget it, to not buy the property. This would have allowed the shortsightedness of the loan officer to interfere with my plans. Obviously, I didn't let this happen, but the fact that the possibility had even crossed my mind meant it *could* have happened. It's similar to how I've reacted to adversity in the past. Trouble my first semester of college? Think about packing it in. Not drafted until the seventh round? Think about packing it in. Team not willing to play me even though I was healthy? Think about packing it in. And now, once again, a new challenge: Not getting a loan? See my previous answers.

I did not walk away, of course, because that feeling of anger and frustration passed, and, just like I've faced every challenge in life, my eventual reaction was to double down and finish what I started. What begins as doubt always ends up being determination, for me, anyway. I'll show them, right? So I explored other options, figured out how to solve my problem, and found the loan somewhere else. I accomplished what I wanted to accomplish.

Another important lesson: just because someone tells you "no" doesn't mean you should take it as the final answer. There's almost always another option. Keep seeking the opportunities that are out there for you. Don't let someone else kill your dream.

Here's one more: I always thought that if you had money, you were good. I didn't know that the world doesn't really work that way. It's not just that you need to have money, it's *how* you have it and what you look like and what you want to do with it. This is a hard lesson to accept.

My rental properties all were booked up pretty quickly, immediately giving me another revenue stream, which means my plan was already paying dividends. I had also just gotten my real estate license and found a broker named Carol Drake, at United Real Estate, who let me work under her. I also talked to my agent, Tony Paige, because I knew there were other players who were looking for houses. Tony hooked me up with one of his other clients, Eric Rowe, of the Miami Dolphins. It took me a while, but eventually I found Eric a house, he bought it, and now I'm on my way. I don't have more clients yet, but other guys have reached out saying they're going to be interested in buying a house in the next year or two. So I keep myself available for them when they need me.

I could hang out a shingle and advertise as a realtor, but I don't want to. Not at the moment, anyway. The key is that I have *options*. All these things I do? They give me options. The more options I have, the better. Something to think about.

The point of all this is I am now a businessman, making my money work for me. The way I did it was by getting myself— no, *pushing myself*—out of my comfort zone. Our brains are wired to repeat the same patterns, so it's hard to step outside of that and do things that aren't comfortable. I had to get out of that mindset because football was comfortable and it was the only thing I had ever done. Jumping into real estate was unfamiliar, but I knew it was the best way to get started as a businessman. I also knew that I'd have to do something I didn't like, which was ask for help, because there was so much I didn't know. I got it from Rene West, as well as Carol, who brought me in to work as a realtor under her umbrella.

People like to glide along a certain path because it's easy and because it feels familiar. I was scared to take on something new, but I did it because I was committed to helping myself and because I enjoy learning new things. That's why I didn't give up when that first loan fell through and ultimately why I ended up going to business school at the University of Houston. In one of my leadership classes there, they talk about the three Cs: Character, Competence, and Commitment. I always had the character and the commitment—what I needed, what I was looking for, was the competence. Carol helped me with that as I started sitting down with her every other weekend, asking questions, and talking about the business. She sat me down and helped me work out a plan. She was the one who broke it down for me, the way to separate my personal real estate investments from the stuff I helped others buy, how it would all look, and how it would work. She has taught me a lot, and her knowledge has been invaluable. One of the reasons I'm meeting and exceeding my goals is because I am not afraid to ask questions and then listen to the answers.

In chapter ten, I talked about how much fun it is to spend money and how it's not terribly fun to learn about it but the most fun of all is *making* it. Part of that is putting yourself into a position where others take you seriously. A bank loan officer turned me down for a loan to buy a town house I wanted to use as a rental property because I'm a young Black man. That's a good lesson to take forward, that people will think of me as a pretender if I just show up without any preparation and assume I know everything. That's how you get exposed and get taken. Preparation isn't always fun, but in the long run, it gives you the know-how to get done what you want to get done. Sounds easy, but the truth is people have a hell of a hard time doing it.

You need to take yourself seriously too. Be serious about what you want, and also be serious about going out there and getting it. Sometimes it's as simple as changing the way you look for a meeting. I don't walk into a bank anymore with sweats on; I wear a nice shirt and slacks and some dress shoes. What's the saying? Don't dress for the job you have, dress for the job you want. I want to be a serious businessman, so I'm going to be one, and I'm going to do all the work that is needed for me to be successful at it, including looking like one.

My transition from the NFL to real life—and let's face it, while pro football is real, it isn't "real life" in the way that most people think of it—wasn't totally easy. It's important to realize that my successful transition wasn't a piece of cake. It took work and planning and effort. It's important for people to know how much went into it and how much goes into *any* major transition. These things don't just happen automatically. You have to decide to go after it, then go after it. It's like my getting my MBA. Again, I'll talk about that in the next chapter, but when it became obvious to me that I didn't know nearly enough to do what I wanted to do, I understood that I had to get out there and learn it.

I'm lucky in that I have the resources to do that. Not everyone does. But the lessons are the same: Set realistic, incremental goals for yourself, and don't try to go out for that one big score. Take things one step at a time. Understand the scope of what you're doing and what your limitations are. Again, this isn't rocket science, but people keep thinking there's an easier way. That's almost never the case.

Do the work, put in the time, take care of the boring and mundane things that need taking care of, even though it's often drudgery. In the long run, it's worth it. I'm in this for keeps, playing the long game. I'm willing to take my time to build something the right way. I'm not just trying to throw stuff together because that leads to trying to do too many things at once, which almost always leads to making mistakes. The better prepared you are, the fewer mistakes you're going to make.

It's that simple.

CHAPTER 13

MBA

I have been asked before why I decided to go back to school to get my MBA. To me, the answer was pretty simple: I realized that I wanted to be a successful businessman but knew very little about business. I didn't really know that much about life either if I'm being honest.

I'd been playing football for twenty years, which had required pretty much all of my focus, and even though I went to a great college, I went there to play football. I've said it before, but it bears repeating: most guys who go to college to play football don't go to college to go to college, they go to play football. While I definitely had to work hard in college, especially at a school like Vanderbilt, the truth was that I was still focusing more on playing than on studying. I have a degree from the university, and I'm incredibly proud of it, but I still didn't really know much and knew I needed to learn more.

I was a college-educated man who was in fact way behind in life, and I knew I wanted to fix that. I *needed* to fix it, so I set about doing that. I already had my real estate license, but that wasn't enough. Not even close.

The process was pretty straightforward. It was May of 2019, and one of my old coaches used to be at the University of Houston (since moved on to the University of Louisiana at Lafayette). I hit him up and asked if he knew anyone in the admissions office at the Houston business school. As it happens, he did, and after I exchanged texts with the person, I was told what to do to get into the fall graduate program at U of H. I took my GREs, got a good score, wrote an essay, went through the whole application process, and the day I did my interview I was accepted into the program. I started my orientation that afternoon. The whole thing came together really fast, which was good because I wanted to kick my higher education into a higher gear.

The orientation was intense. It taught me things I needed to know for school, like how to use the formatting and organizational program Excel, for instance. There were leadership and group exercises, necessary stuff but really long. Once we got into actual school, though, it got better. Not easier, because the classes were really hard, but...more interesting, for sure. My first semester, I took classes on stats, accounting, and finance, and even though I'd just spent six weeks in real estate school and five years in NFL meetings that were, as mentioned, alarmingly similar to taking college classes, it was still a bit of a struggle to find my footing. The stuff they were teaching me was over my head at first. I mean, I couldn't even comprehend it.

But remember when I was hesitant to approach other students at Vanderbilt because I was scared of what they would think of me? Well, I didn't have that problem here. We had all been in orientation together, and I wasn't some football player skating by on scholarship; I was in the same program as everyone else, having earned my spot there. So instead of suffering through this on my own, I met with others, I talked to people about our classes, I asked for help. People were fantastic, happy to help, interested in working together. It was like, "I got you, man!" It was a relief, actually, knowing I could count on and work with others to accomplish my goals. It was a great example of taking the things I'd learned, the wisdom I'd attained over the years, and actually putting them to work to accomplish new things. It's one thing to gain wisdom—it's another to apply it to help yourself.

Another difference was that the classes in business school, aside from being more difficult than the undergrad classes at Vandy, were *required*. I had a few electives here and there, but most of the classes I was taking were mandatory requirements of the program. This helped force me out of my comfort zone, which is something I've needed help with in the past. I know it's good for me—it's almost always good for anyone who does it, to get out of your comfort zone—but that doesn't mean it's easy. That's probably why it's called the "comfort zone"—because being outside of it is not comfortable, regardless of how helpful it might be.

Today I get up and talk in front of people, and I do it with confidence. I work with others. I keep my mind open to all kinds of new thoughts and new knowledge that I didn't used to, and all of this is helping me grow not just financially but on a personal and emotional level too. The whole process has helped me in every aspect of my life. For instance, I took a class on business decision-making, and this class has affected the way I think about everything. One of the books was called *Flow* by Mihaly Csikszentmihalyi and was about how you can utilize your "flow state" to make better decisions and remain in the zone—avoiding the noise that might have a negative effect on you while also recognizing what that noise is, how to identify it, how to find success in spite of it, and how to move forward rather than being pushed back.

Don't get me wrong. I think my decision-making process has always been pretty good, but to suggest that it couldn't get better, that it couldn't be molded and shaped a bit, is just arrogant, and that's one thing I'm not. I've been through too much and worked too hard to expect that I am owed anything other than what I've earned, so arrogance tends to aggravate me and is not something I ever want to be accused of.

Obviously, there's the other nitty-gritty stuff too. Learning to read a spreadsheet, being able to analyze things I couldn't before, using skills I knew I would pick up in the program. It's also helping me to refine my business interests moving forward. I realize that I'm not interested in finance, in pushing money around—I want to be involved in things that are more tangible. Real estate is a good example of that, but if I'm going to be investing in other businesses, I want them to be making something, creating things for people to use or consume. I want to make an impact, and, look, if there's a way to make a few bucks while I'm at it, there's nothing wrong with that.

I've talked before about having goals and that I want to have a multiunit building before the end of the year, but long term, aside from being involved in meaningful businesses, I like the idea of owning something bigger, maybe a complex with several hundred units, and to be able to break down those numbers—the units, the rents, the supplies and upkeep, the water and power, the number of employees on site, the insurance costs, and so on—this is the kind of thing training and formal education get you, the ability to handle all that. To me, it's part of my ongoing quest to educate myself as much as I possibly can.

On top of that, there's the networking aspect. Part of going through a program like this is getting the opportunity to meet other like-minded people who want to succeed in business as well. You can't just hop into commercial real estate and be really good at it the moment you begin. It takes work and experience, and being able to work with others who have that experience will only be a benefit. I am twenty-nine years old. I don't expect to know all the answers now, nor do I expect to accomplish everything I want to accomplish right now. It starts now, yes, but there will still be things to accomplish when I am thirty and thirty-five and forty on up.

More than anything else, I think business school is teaching me a process. If I want to get from point A to point Z, I can't just skip all the steps in between. I understand that I need to be able to enact each of the other necessary steps along the way. That's how you become really successful. It's not about doing it fast; it's about doing it right. If you do it right, it'll last longer. Doing it fast will get it done quicker, obviously, but even if you get to where you're going, you might not even remember how you got there, and odds are the thing you built won't sustain. You lose a lot of information by going too fast. Taking your time, going step-by-step, is a better way.

Knowing what I don't know is important. It's another thing that is worth repeating. Don't assume that asking questions makes you look weak; it actually makes you look smart. Because when you do it, you're saying, "I'm not going to be a mark here. I'm not going to have somebody take advantage of me because I'm afraid to ask questions." So it's the same concept here—I am being methodical. I'm not just saying, "I need to have this incredible success," and then go do it. It's more like, I'm going to get there, but I have to go through these steps first, and I want to know that by the time I get to that point, I'll be ready for it. I'll be prepared. I'll be knowledgeable.

You might wonder why it's so important to me to do well in school rather than just use it to learn what I need and move on to bigger things. Well, certainly part of it is that you have to maintain a 3.0 GPA to even stay in the program. But that's an external reason. The internal reason is that it's important to me to do a job well. If I'm going to be involved in something like this, if I'm going to be a part of this kind of program, I want to get the most out of it that I possibly can. Why bother otherwise? There's so much here to help me, I want to absorb it all. The financial understanding, the accounting skills, the knowledge of economics and everything that goes with that. It's all part of the same thing, and it's all really valuable. It will be even more valuable once I start working toward something bigger. I know that having those skills will come in handy. But more than that, having these skills will help me reach and exceed my goals.

Having said all that, and as hard as the classes are, it's definitely easier to pick things up now than it was in college. Maybe that's because I don't have to focus any of my energy on football. Also, because I really am working harder. Whereas before I might have been okay with a C, now working hard is not only necessary for me to stay in the program, it's necessary for me psychologically.

Side note: the NFL Players Association (NFLPA) has a program for players after they retire that reimburses us for higher education expenses. It's meant to encourage guys like me to be successful after our football careers are complete, and I'm taking full advantage of it. There is one program where they cover tuition, but because I felt like I wanted to have something on the line, I put my own money out first, and I'll eventually get reimbursed by the league. In order to qualify, you need to have a C average or above, but since that's lower than the program requirement, it's sort of moot. Still, the motivation is there to complete it all. I probably would have done this anyway, even without the NFLPA, simply because I knew my education wasn't anywhere near complete. But since it's there, why not take advantage of it?

I know a lot of guys in the league have no interest in this after they retire, and that's a shame because it's a valuable resource. I didn't want to go to school, I didn't want to go to college to actually learn anything, and I think most guys are probably like that. I just wanted to go play football, which is pretty much par for the course. But things change. Football got old and ended. There was a lot of my life left to live, and

I wanted to know as much as I possibly could to live it right. The fact that this opportunity is available but there are guys who don't take advantage of it is sort of a shame, but I wasn't going to be one of them. If I had the chance to tell guys about this—and sometimes I do—I would tell them to do it. Not only do you not have anything to lose, you have everything to gain.

This is especially true when you consider how many players finish their careers and then, a couple years later, are totally broke. It doesn't have to be that way. Remember what I said in chapter ten about how it's not really fun to learn about money? Well, I also said the most fun is making it, and it's tough to do the one without the other.

Still, it's hard to convince people of something, especially when they've already convinced themselves of something else. Unfortunate, but true.

This won't stop me from talking to guys in the league after I get my graduate degree, of course. I mean, since I'm slowly getting more comfortable talking to groups of people and all. But it's something guys need to know about, these programs, because they're out there, but they're not used very much. That's another shame because most guys are out of the league while they're still in their twenties, and most everyone else (unless your name is Tom Brady or Drew Brees) is out in their thirties. That's a lot of life left to live, so why not grab an opportunity like this when it's presented to you? The average career of an NFL player is around three years. Less than the time a normal person spends in college. Think about that.

Planning ahead is a good thing. Most guys don't do it, but it's not that hard. People are often lazy, but it doesn't take much to come up with a plan and set it in motion. Sometimes it's as easy as just doing something that's good for you, and that starts you down the road to more things just like it. When I started meditating my second year in the league, I didn't do it with an eye toward retiring, I did it because I knew I needed focus. But it helped me with things down the road and opened the door to yoga and to developing a better understanding about myself and my life.

On the other hand, sometimes life throws you a curveball, and it's how you react to crises that makes all the difference. Cancer kept me out of the game and made me realize there's more to life than football. It allowed me to envision a life away from it for the first time. I finish the season, I'm lost, I start having conversations with a couple of yoga instructors who don't know that I'm a football player; they just see me as Dre. It dawns on me that maybe people really will see me outside of shoulder pads and a helmet. Maybe that part of my life is realistic. Then I go to Headspace and get more comfortable out in the real world and away from football. All of these little things add up to being confident that walking away from the game is the right decision.

I have done quite well in the two-plus years since I retired, at least partially because I was prepared. I took the time to learn new things and to be careful, and that's exactly what I'm doing now. I got a head start, and now I'm trying to set myself up for the future by spending time doing something that is really, really hard but in the long run will make my life easier.

Everybody eventually walks away from the game. Time, as they say, is undefeated. It's inevitable. With that in mind, it's silly to live in denial, to think that you can hold it off forever, to think you don't have to be ready for when that day comes. When I finish school, I'll talk to guys in the league and be up front about that. It's not usually something people want to hear, but then, that's life. We're told things we don't want to hear all the time. In this case, I'm here to tell you something that'll actually help you because I can speak from experience. It's all about protecting yourself. Getting my MBA is just another part of that.

There's another aspect to this too, and it ties in with so many of the other things I've discussed throughout this book. Going to school and getting a master's degree has given me more insight into my life and myself. Life really is about confidence, and there are always more chances to get that if you need it. I continue to need it, and while the victories I've achieved over time—both large and small— have strengthened my confidence, I'm still a young man. I still need reinforcement. After a lifetime of being unsure whether I was smart enough to fit into a world outside of football—first academic, then professional, and now academic again—knowing that I'm one of the gang here, that I fit in with this group as well as anyone else, is enough to tell me I can do anything.

The instinct says I just got off a football field and there's no way I can hang with these people in this program. The reality is different. It's the opposite, in fact, and so whatever doubts I have, whatever doubts that continue after I dispel them over and over again, they are dispelled once more by the experience. I can make it because I *am* making it. Realizing that sitting in a football meeting room and going to class are not so different certainly helps. So does acceptance from others and getting good grades. Add them all together, and it's about shifting your mindset so that you're able to succeed, enjoying that success instead of constantly second-guessing yourself, and allowing yourself to appreciate what you've done.

I don't know if people ever actually set out to be a role model, and I don't know if it's appropriate to ask to be one, but I know the Texans asked me to come and talk to their rookies, which I am going to do, and I intend to talk to other players too. I have valuable lessons I've learned that I think can help them, if they're willing to listen.

CHAPTER 14

What's Next

S o now where does that leave us? I've told you all about my life, the lessons I've learned, and the transitions I've made, and a good part of that time I've spent talking about my plans for the future. You know me, you know my plans, you know my goals, which begs the question: What else can I tell you?

Turns out, a few things.

My life is a lot different now from what I thought it would be. Before I was diagnosed with cancer, if you'd asked me what I'd be doing at twenty-nine, I'd have told you, "Playing football." There wouldn't have been a doubt in my mind. That was the plan, and there wasn't any reason to think it wouldn't continue to be. But that's the thing about plans is that they're fluid. The old cliché says, "Man plans, God laughs," and it's actually true. You can't make a plan and expect it to go flawlessly simply because there are too many external forces at work, and they're almost always working against you. For me, it was cancer and then my father dying, and suddenly that plan of mine wasn't so set in stone anymore.

So when I talk about my current plans—like the things I want to accomplish over the coming months and years—there is a fluidity to it, a flexibility to deal with any of those unforeseen external forces that might interfere. A good plan has to have space to evolve or else it's not a good plan. That, or everything goes perfectly, but how often does that happen? Pretty much never in my experience.

Since I'm in business school at the University of Houston, for instance, that has become my priority. So if I don't accomplish some of the more business-oriented goals I've had in mind but I continue to flourish with my master's degree education, I will count that as a win and simply add the unfulfilled goals to my life after I have that MBA in my hand. The end result will be the same because eventually I'll fulfill those goals, but the time line changes because the plan changed. It had to because my life and priorities did. That's another thing that carries over into pretty much all other parts of life, the need to adapt when situations change and staying resilient when they do.

For now, I want to focus on real estate, though I know that will change, as I will eventually want to branch out. Maybe invest in a restaurant or a few of them. But at the moment, where I stand feels like a good fit for me. I like the minutiae of finding the right place and doing the research to make sure it fits all of my parameters. And once you have a few, you want more, and the more you get, the bigger the business gets.

That's why I'm in business school now, so that I can learn how to manage everything I know that I want to acquire.

But at the same time, I also understand that fulfilling the goal just to fulfill it—like buying a property that isn't right for me just so I can cross something off a list—is a mistake. The only thing that matters is what will benefit me and my business, and this is something people don't always understand. Like it's somehow more important to say you did something than it is to wait and make sure you did it right. That goes hand in hand with being able to adjust on the fly. Just look at what happened with me and football. I planned on having a great year and maybe going on to the Pro Bowl, winning a Super Bowl. Then boom, cancer. Boom, dad dies. Boom, football is over. Boom, time for a new plan.

These are extreme examples of things that were out of my control, but they make the point. Life, goals, plans, they all have to factor that stuff in and evolve accordingly. So now the goals are broader and more long term, like getting more properties until I get to the point where I'm ready for a really large building with at least one hundred units. That's not something I can jump into, but I can build up to it and get there within a few years. I'm twenty-nine, so I have time. I'm lucky in that aspect, but I know I'm lucky, and not only do I not take it for granted, I actually take advantage of it because I know I'm ahead of the curve. I know I don't need to rush. The journey is important. I know I'll make mistakes, but if I'm careful and take things as they come, I'll be able to keep those mistakes to a minimum. Equally important, I'll be able to learn from the ones I'm still going to make. It's an important way to think and an important way to navigate through life.

Goals can be about more than work too. I have personal goals, of course, like continuing to try to improve as a person and a man. The meditation, the yoga, the intent to read and learn and educate myself, these have all contributed greatly to my personal growth. The focus I bring to school and to the business side I also bring to myself because I believe that the two go hand in hand. If you know yourself, if you strive to be better, then it will transfer to your professional life. For so many years, football was the only thing that mattered. I was a good person, but I wasn't all that intellectually curious. But as I phased football out of my life, the void was filled with things that are, without question, far more constructive and healthier. When I say healthy, I mean physically, of course, but also emotionally, psychologically, and spiritually. Wanting to be successful in business is important, but to me, if I am not also successful as a human being, then it won't mean anything.

I spent twenty years of my life focusing on football but never cared that much about it. It was a means to an end. Even when I was a kid, I recognized that it was about maintaining a bond with my dad. And if my dad had been a big baseball fan, I might be playing for the Astros now. But even though that was me for most of my life, I have a hard time recognizing that guy anymore because it feels like so long ago, like a different person entirely. Now that I'm free of football—and yes, I still think of it in those terms—I won't ever again do something I don't really want to do. If it doesn't really hit me deep inside, I won't do it. It took me a while to get to this point, and I know a lot of people never get there, but it is possible, even if you never see a million dollars in your life. It's not about money. Well, it's not entirely about money, because I know some people feel trapped due to their financial situation, but my point is that if you work hard enough and dedicate yourself to making a change, you can do it. It's about will.

I don't say any of this lightly. If you've read this far, I'd like to think you understand that. These are lessons learned from adversity, from facing tough times and getting through them. Now, having been through it and having come out the other side, I push myself to be better, to do better, and to improve. I said I barely recognize the old person I used to be, the football player, and my hope is that when I turn thirty-five, then forty, and continue to get older, I'll continue evolving and won't be able to recognize the man I am now either.

People don't really change, but they can evolve. I think most people stay the same, whether they like themselves or not, because it's easier that way. I don't like easy. I spent many years of my life doing the easy stuff. Honestly, the tough stuff is more interesting. The tough stuff brings about the greatest growth.

You know what? Life is hard. For most people, just getting through it is enough. It shouldn't be. People are often their own worst enemies simply because they take the easy way out or they make quick, careless decisions that end up working against them. It doesn't have to be that way. It only takes focus and the willingness to work at it. To put in the time and the effort to make it better. To make yourself better.

But Andre, you might ask, how do I do that? Honestly? It's not as hard as you think. It does take effort, which is where some people get immediately tripped up.

Start with yourself. Start seeing who you are and visualizing who you want to be. See how you feel about a certain thing, and then go from there. It's a process. You don't just snap your fingers and change. It's a gradual evolution. Who you are as a person—like whether you're angry or sad, if you're funny or serious, if you're selfish or generous, for instance—doesn't tend to change. But behavior does. Attitude does. Mindset does. How you react to things and how you treat others, this is stuff that you can't just change overnight. It takes work. It takes thoughtfulness and introspection. That's not always pleasant, but it sure is necessary. The work you put in will definitely change you. Again, I know from experience, and I wasn't actively trying to change myself while I was doing it. I just found myself doing work that I knew would help me, and it led to bigger and better things.

The truth is, in a sense, change was forced on me. I could have resisted it, but it would have made me miserable. What it did was make me ask why I thought a certain way or why I did a certain thing. Do I really love football? No, I don't, but if I hadn't had cancer, I'd still be playing. If my dad were alive, I'd still be playing. If I were a bigger star, I'd still be playing. Those are three big things, but they did happen, and I'm no longer in the NFL. Take it one step further and it led to my making these changes in my life that include writing this book and opening myself up in a way I never have previously and never could have before all this happened. I'm a private person. Something like this would not only never have interested me before, it wouldn't have even occurred to me.

Before all that stuff happened, I was just chilling. Nothing all that big had ever happened to me, so it was just living a day-by-day existence, thinking about football without much thought about the future.

Then, suddenly, football wasn't as important, and it led to me understanding I was about more than that. I had to start asking questions about who I was, about what I wanted, and that's what ultimately leads to change or at least evolution. The cancer reminded me that football was not forever—a relief I didn't realize I felt until later—which allowed me to end it sooner than I would have. By ending that part of my life, I found it became necessary to figure out who I was in the next part. It's a journey I'm still taking, with answers I'm still seeking and change I'm still making.

The big lesson that hit home for me then is that life is about more than one thing. For it to be meaningful, it must be multidimensional. Because that's really what it comes down to: so many people get so caught up in one particular thing and find themselves blinded to everything else. They think, "If not for this thing, *what* am I? If not for this thing, *who* am I?" But guess what? You're more than that one thing, just like I realized I was more than football. Walking away from it, finding a life apart from it, friends who didn't know about my involvement in it, acceptance from those who didn't connect me to it, all of those things reassured me that I was more than football and am more than football. It was just a big part of my life, and now that it's over I can move on and replace it with other things that become important to me, none of which will define me.

Walking away gives you power. There's no other way to say it. It's empowering in a way you'll never expect, and I know this because I didn't expect to feel the way I did when I walked away. The truth is, I didn't really know who I was when I did it. I still don't, but I'm figuring it out, one day at a time.

When I think of the future now, that's pretty much how I think of it. One day at a time. Not in the way I did before, where I wasn't thinking about bigger things or grander goals or plans, but rather because I'm staying present and staying centered. Goals remain the same, sure, but now I face them—and embrace them—with a much stronger awareness of everything. Someday I'd like to get married and have kids of my own, but that's down the road and not on my immediate radar. That will come when it comes, and just like everything else, I'm not in any rush to get there. Planning ten years in the future is good in a grand sense in the way that you can tell yourself that you want to be roughly in a certain place and have certain things, but it's also limiting because if they don't happen exactly the way you want them to, where does it leave you? What's important is working every day to improve myself and become a better human being.

The quest to find myself, to really figure out who Andre Hal is—really who *Dre* is—will continue. It has to. I'll keep learning things on this journey, keep trying to get better, keep seeking and striving and doing better. Or trying to. Aspiring to.

We should all aspire to be better and to find out who we are, for better or worse. Sometimes that involves walking away from the only thing you know, sometimes it involves taking a step you didn't know you could take, and sometimes it means asking yourself questions you don't have the answers to.

I think that if I've learned anything, it's that the answers come when you try to seek them. That's part of life, you know? It's filled with trials and tribulations, but in the end, it's the seeking, the being, the doing, the living, that really makes it interesting.

And we all want to be seekers and doers, right?

About the Author

Former NFL safety Andre Hal began his career on a football scholarship at Vanderbilt University. As a sophomore, Andre began a three-year streak as a cornerback starter for the Commodores, going to three consecutive bowl games for the first time in Vanderbilt history.

In 2014, Andre was a seventh-round draft pick and signed a four-year contract with the Houston Texans. In his second year, he switched to playing safety, became a starter mid-season, and eventually signed a new deal with the team in 2017.

Since retiring from the NFL, Andre has built a successful career in real estate. He lives in Houston, Texas.